# Toward
## the
# Goal

## Other Books in the
## Zonderkidz Biography Series

*The Admiral: The David Robinson Story*

*Beyond the Music: The Bono Story*

*Defender of Faith: The Mike Fisher Story*

*Driven by Faith: The Trevor Bayne Story*

*Gifted Hands: The Ben Carson Story*

*Gift of Peace: The Jimmy Carter Story*

*Heart of a Champion: The Dominique Dawes Story*

*Linspired: The Jeremy Lin Story*

*Man on a Mission: The David Hilmer Story*

*Prophet with Honor: The Billy Graham Story*

*Reaching New Heights: The Kelly Clark Story*

*Speed to Glory: The Cullen Jones Story*

### Hardcover Autobiographies

*Game Changer: Faith, Football, and Finding Your Way*
by Kirk Cousins

*Grace, Gold, & Glory: My Leap of Faith*
By Gabrielle Douglas with Michelle Burford

*Through My Eyes: A Quarterback's Journey*
By Tim Tebow with Nathan Whitaker

# Toward the Goal

## the
## Kaká Story
### REVISED EDITION

**Jeremy V. Jones**
**&**
**Janna Jones**

ZONDERKIDZ

*Toward the Goal, Revised Edition*
Copyright © 2010, 2014 by Jeremy V. Jones

This title is also available as a Zondervan ebook.
Visit www.zondervan.com/ebooks.

Requests for information should be addressed to:

Zondervan, 3900 *Sparks Drive SE, Grand Rapids, Michigan 49546*

ISBN: 978-0-310-73840-4

All Scripture quotations, unless otherwise indicated, are taken from The Holy Bible,
*New International Version®, NIV®.* Copyright © 1973, 1978, 1984, 2011 by Biblica, Inc.®
Used by permission. All rights reserved worldwide.

*Cover design: Kris Nelson*
*Cover photography: Jeff Mitchell-FIFA/Getty Images*
*Interior design: Ben Fetterley and Greg Johnson/Textbook Perfect*

*Printed in the United States of America*

20  21  /DCI/  22  21  20  19  18  17  16  15  14  13  12  11  10  9  8  7  6

# Contents

1. A Champion Among Champions . . . . . . . . . . . . 7
2. A Boy in Brazil . . . . . . . . . . . . . . . . . . . . . . 13
3. Jogo Bonito . . . . . . . . . . . . . . . . . . . . . . . . . 20
4. God and Soccer . . . . . . . . . . . . . . . . . . . . . . 26
5. The Accident . . . . . . . . . . . . . . . . . . . . . . . . 32
6. Instant *Craque*. . . . . . . . . . . . . . . . . . . . . . . 38
7. Sudden Fame . . . . . . . . . . . . . . . . . . . . . . . . 43
8. The Yellow and Green . . . . . . . . . . . . . . . . . . 48
9. World Champion . . . . . . . . . . . . . . . . . . . . . . 54
10. Europe Calling. . . . . . . . . . . . . . . . . . . . . . . 61
11. Benvenuti in Italia . . . . . . . . . . . . . . . . . . . . 66
12. Learning the Hard Way . . . . . . . . . . . . . . . . . 71
13. Radical Reputation . . . . . . . . . . . . . . . . . . . . 77
14. Not-So-Magic in Germany . . . . . . . . . . . . . . . 83
15. Golden Year. . . . . . . . . . . . . . . . . . . . . . . . . 90
16. Not About the Money . . . . . . . . . . . . . . . . . . 99
17. Champions Heading for the World Cup . . . . . . 107
18. Reality at Real . . . . . . . . . . . . . . . . . . . . . . . 114
19. Back to the World Cup. . . . . . . . . . . . . . . . . . 121
20. Sidelined by Surgery . . . . . . . . . . . . . . . . . . . 128
21. Ups and Downs — For Kaká and Club . . . . . . . 137
22. Hope . . . . . . . . . . . . . . . . . . . . . . . . . . . . . . 143
23. Toward the Goal . . . . . . . . . . . . . . . . . . . . . . 148

*For Mom and Dad—*

For the orange slices, clean jerseys, bug repellent, registration fees, practice transportations, and encouragement during my own days on the field. Thank you for introducing me to the beautiful game—and most of all for your unwavering support through all the game of life.

JVJ

# A Champion Among Champions

It was the biggest game of the year. The winner would be the champion of all of Europe's mighty professional leagues and teams. Soccer clubs across the continent had played each other all season long in the ongoing UEFA Champions League tournament. Now, on May 23, 2007 in approximately ninety minutes of soccer, Italy's AC Milan or England's Liverpool would be crowned the best of the best.

Police in riot gear ringed the outside of Olympic Stadium in Athens, Greece. At one point fans without tickets tried to break down a closed gate to storm their way, and the police fired tear gas to repel them.

But the true battle was taking place on the brilliant green grass rectangle at the center of the stadium. Seventy thousand cheering, chanting fans watched as the action unfolded in red and white before them. Milan wore white; Liverpool red.

Liverpool took control of the action early, and the Reds' Jermaine Pennant got the first shot on goal eight minutes in. But Milan's goalkeeper, Dida, made the diving save.

Once Milan settled down, the game was evenly matched, and neither side could break through the other's tough defense. It seemed as if the two coaches had prepared their teams so well that the defenses could anticipate every attack.

The Milan team was filled with veteran World Cup winners and European Champions such as Paolo Maldini and Clarence Seedorf, but its superstar was young number twenty-two: Kaká. It was his heroic play in the semifinal game that had secured the victory over Manchester United and propelled the *Rossoneri* (Milan's nickname, referring to their red and black uniforms) to this final game.

Liverpool was well aware of the threat Kaká posed and used its defensive midfielder Javier Mascherano to dog Milan's most creative playmaker and pressure him constantly. The tactic seemed to work. Kaká and his whole team mustered only one shot on goal during the first half, and it was easily saved by Liverpool's keeper Pepe Reina.

A minute before halftime, Kaká was fouled just outside of Liverpool's penalty area, giving a free kick to Milan. Their free kick specialist Andrea Pirlo placed the silver and blue-starred game ball on the turf twenty-three yards from the goal in the center of the field. Ten yards back, Liverpool lined up eight men in a wall to create a barrier. Anticipation grew as the fans knew that set plays like this were always dangerous opportunities for a team to score a goal. Would this one put Milan ahead at halftime? Would the Milan shooter go straight for the goal, looking for a way around Liverpool's wall? Or would he pass to a teammate who could take a quick shot from another angle?

Milan's striker Filippo Inzaghi had lined up on the edge of Liverpool's wall. As soon as Pirlo struck the ball, he turned and sprinted toward the goal. The shot bent around the inside edge of the wall, curling toward the left side of the goal. Goalkeeper Reina dove to his left and looked like he would cover the shot. But as Inzaghi turned to look back, the ball struck him on the shoulder and deflected back toward the other side of the goal, behind Reina. Goal Milan!

The goal gave Milan momentum that they carried into the second half, pressing their attack as Liverpool's defense began to weaken. The score remained 1–0, however, until the final ten minutes.

In an effort to come from behind as the end of the game approached, Liverpool substituted in another attacker to try to come up with an equalizing goal. Liverpool's Mascherano went out, and Kaká quickly made the most of the opportunity. Shaking Mascherano's shadow, Kaká quickly found some freedom and space on the field. Right away he chipped a pass to Inzaghi in front of the open goal, but the striker couldn't get the shot on goal.

A few minutes later, Kaká received a pass and dribbled the ball with lots of open space toward Liverpool's goal box, shuffled subtly as if he might shoot, then sent a crisp through-ball between three defenders. Inzaghi rushed through from across the center and had only the goalie between him and net. With one touch he pushed the ball toward the baseline to avoid the charging Reina. Then, from a difficult angle, he sent the ball rolling beneath the goalie's dive, across the goal mouth, and into the opposite side net. Goal!

Inzaghi ran to the corner and grabbed the corner flag. He fell to his knees pumping his fists and shouting, then lowered his face to the ground. Kaká was the first teammate to run and embrace him. Milan had a 2–0 lead.

Liverpool attacked desperately and received a corner kick in the eighty-ninth minute. The ball sailed in to the near corner of the goal box. It was headed across the goal toward Dirk Kuyt near the far post, and Kuyt headed the ball into the back of the net to cut the lead in half.

Two years ago these very same teams had faced off in the 2005 Champions League final. AC Milan took a 3–0 lead into halftime, only to see the Liverpool unbelievably fight back to send the game into a shootout tiebreaker, then win on penalty kicks. Could the Reds find another miracle comeback?

But time was on Milan's side in this game, and the referee blew his final whistle three minutes later. The Rossoneri were the champions of Europe and arguably of the whole world.

The Italian fans went wild, and Liverpool fans cried. Kaká and his teammates celebrated joyously, and fans cheered and sang in the stands as confetti rained onto the field. Kaká stripped off his jersey to reveal a white T-shirt

Kaká celebrates after beating Liverpool 2-1 to win the Champions League Final soccer match, May 23, 2007.

Associated Press/Murad Sezer

with big black lettering that said "I belong to Jesus" in English. The Brazilian star ran a victory lap around the field cheering and waving both arms to the fans as a cluster of cameramen and photographers tried to keep up. Finally, Milan was presented with the huge silver cup.

The victory completed an amazing year for Kaká, but there were even more accolades to come. Many sports magazines had been calling Kaká the best player in the world. In October he was officially named the Federation Internationale des Associations de Footballeurs Professionnels (FIFPro) 2007 World Player of the Year, voted on by more than forty-five thousand soccer professionals around the world.

In December he received the prestigious Ballon d'Or, or Golden Ball, for the best player in the world by *France Football* magazine. And later that month, Kaká was voted the FIFA World Player of the Year by the world's national team coaches and captains.

"It's really special for me—it was a dream for me just to play for São Paulo and one game for Brazil," Kaká said when he accepted the golden trophy. "But the Bible says God can give you more than you even ask for, and that is what has happened in my life."

Kaká had been dreaming big since he was a boy, and his faith had carried him even when the odds seemed long that he would ever become a soccer player. But with hard work, determination, and humility he had reached great heights. This is the story of how it all happened— and how he continues to persevere to stay at the top of the soccer world.

# A Boy in Brazil

Ricardo Izecson dos Santos Leite was known as Ricardinho, which means Little Richard or Ricky, for the earliest years of his life. But when his younger brother, Digão, began learning to speak, he couldn't pronounce his brother's name. Kaká (pronounced *ka-KA*) was the best he could do, and the name stuck.

The boys were both born in Brasília, the capital of Brazil. The city had only been built in 1960, when President Juscelino Kubitschek ordered the capital to be moved from the Atlantic coast to the country's interior savanna region. The nation's constitution had called for the capital to be moved closer to the nation's center as early as 1891. But the world-famous city Rio de Janeiro had remained the seat of the government. City planners laid out Brasília carefully, and from high up in the sky the center of the metropolis looks like an airplane or a bird.

Kaká and Digão knew the place simply as home. Their father, Bosca Izecson Pereira Leite, was a civil engineer, and their mother, Simone Cristina Santos Leite, a teacher. Both parents loved them very much and took good care of their sons.

Mr. Leite's job brought a move to Cuiabá, a city about six hundred miles west of Brasília, when Kaká was four. The family moved to São Paulo when Kaká was seven years old, and this city became their permanent home.

Kaká began attending school at the Colegio Baptista Brasileiro, or Brazilian Baptist School. He was a calm, shy kid in school. He was an excellent student who earned good grades, and his teachers hoped that he might grow up one day to be a doctor or engineer.

Like most boys his age, he also enjoyed sports. He loved bodyboarding and trying to surf when his family vacationed at the beach. At home, tennis was his favorite for a while, and he dreamed of winning professional tennis tournaments one day. That was before he got serious about soccer, or *futebol* as it's called in Brazil.

Kaká's first memory of soccer is of going with his father to watch São Paulo play when he was eight. At school he began playing *futsal*, a Brazilian version of indoor soccer played with a smaller ball. That same year a P.E. teacher named Enio told Mr. and Mrs. Leite that they should enroll their son in a special soccer academy. They took his advice and signed Kaká up for a soccer club. In a Brazilian TV story years later, Enio remembered him being better at handling a soccer ball than

Globo via Getty Images

Kaká started playing soccer at a young age. Here he plays with a ball in his house in Brazil.

most of the kids, but still being patient with those who weren't as talented as he was.

Mr. Leite also paid for a membership to train at the São Paulo Football Club's facilities. Like teams in Europe, professional soccer teams in Brazil have their own academies. They even have youth teams so they can coach and develop children's soccer talents. As competition gets tougher as age groups rise, the clubs watch for special talent and hope to find their future professional players.

Founded in 1935, São Paulo FC had a long, rich history. It is the most successful club in Brazil, according to the number of championship titles they've received, and is considered the third most popular club behind Flamengo and Corinthians.

The club takes its name from the city where it's located. São Paulo is Brazil's largest metropolis. In fact, it has one of the largest populations in the entire world, with about 20 million people in its metropolitan area. The differences between São Paulo and Rio de Janeiro have been compared to the rivalry between American cities Los Angeles and New York City. Like Los Angeles, Rio is set in a beautiful coastal and natural setting; it is famous for its flamboyant *Carnaval* celebrations, big glitzy parties, and parades. São Paulo is more like New York, and is known for its art, culture, and sophistication. It is often described as having a European flavor.

Brazil itself is the fifth-largest nation in the world, with nearly 200 million people. Like many South American countries there is a great deal of poverty. Living conditions for working class citizens are considered impoverished by Western standards. Most people fall into either the poor or wealthy classes, with a very small middle class in between.

São Paulo is a wealthier city in general, and São Paulo FC was traditionally known as the team of the upper classes. By comparison, Corinthians was founded by members of São Paulo's working class and has maintained strong support from that sector of the population.

Kaká's family was financially comfortable because both of his parents were well-educated professionals. They were able to pay for Kaká's soccer academy tuition and provide him with good opportunities to sharpen his skills, but he would still have to prove himself on the field if he wanted to progress.

Besides, at the time, Kaká was unaware of the social structures around him. He was simply a young boy playing a fun game.

## One Name Wonders

Kaká, Ronaldo, Pelé, Ronaldinho, Dida, Lucio, Fred ... the list of Brazilian players who go by only one name goes on and on. So what's with the one name? It's not only a tradition of Brazilian soccer players; many people in Brazil go by only one name. It's so common that some phone books in Brazil even list them that way rather than by their full names. The one name can be the person's first name, last name, a contraction of the two, or a completely unrelated nickname. Referring to someone by their first name or nickname is a sign of close friendship. In Brazil, calling someone by his nickname shows both care and respect for the person.

There is no definitive answer for where the tradition began. Some say it could have roots in a traditional high illiteracy rate — people went by one shorter name to avoid spelling and writing the full name. Others say the tradition may date back to the time of slavery, when slaves were often recorded and called by only one name. What's certain is that the tradition today is all about personality and individuality. And Brazil's fans love the closeness they feel with players they call by one name.

While Brazil is best known for the tradition, other countries with a large number of one-name players include Portugal, Spain, and Angola.

## Brazil

Brazil, or Brasil as it's spelled in Portuguese, is the largest country in South America, covering nearly half of the continent and bordering all South American countries except Chile and Ecuador. Its neighbors to the north are Venezuela, Guyana, Suriname, and French Guiana. It's bordered to the northeast, east, and southeast by the Atlantic Ocean. To the south is Uruguay, and to the southwest are Argentina and Paraguay. It borders Bolivia and Peru on the west, and Columbia to the northwest. It's the fifth-largest country in the world after Russia, Canada, China, and the United States (when Hawaii, Alaska, and the territories are included).

Prior to the arrival of European explorers, the area that is now Brazil was populated by indigenous groups. Explorers from Portugal arrived in the 1500s and named their new land Brazil after the "pau-brasil" wood from which they made red dye. Brazil was settled by the Portuguese and remains the only Portuguese-speaking country in South America as a result of its colonial history.

The majority of Brazil's 197 million people live in Brazil's capital city of Brasília or in its largest cities, São Paulo and Rio de Janeiro. São Paulo is one of the world's most populous cities with a population of around 19 million people. But while most of the population is concentrated near the coast, the land of Brazil is incredibly diverse. Brazil is framed by two of the world's largest river systems: the Amazon in the north, and the Paraná River in the south. It has the world's largest rain forest but also includes savannah, wetlands, highlands, and the coastal areas.

And Brazil is rich with natural resources. It has the world's largest reserves of fresh water, tropical forest, and biodiversity. In fact, enough water flows out of the Amazon each day to keep New York City supplied for 10 years! Historically much of the land has been exploited, but there have been increased efforts in recent years to preserve and utilize the country's natural resources. While the country still struggles with high crime in areas and unequal distribution of wealth, it is progressing as a nation. By utilizing its vast natural resources and a large labor pool, it has become a regional economic power and leader in South America.

# Jogo Bonita

Almost every young boy in Brazil must dream of being a soccer pro at one time or another. Millions devote themselves to pursuing that dream, playing soccer in streets, fields, beaches, empty lots, jungle clearings, or any area large and flat enough. Many Brazilian fathers give their sons soccer balls in their baby cribs, and most Brazilian children know how to juggle a ball by the time they are three years old.

Poor kids often play barefoot and may not even have a real ball. Instead, they might use a bundle of rags, a sock stuffed with newspapers, or any other round object or ball. Besides being a fun sport they love, soccer allows them to dream of making a better life for themselves.

If a child is good enough, he might be spotted by a local scout in the daily street games and given a tryout with a club team. Or like Kaká, he might be spotted in school and recommended to a club. Or he may simply go to a regional tryout held by a club looking for talented players. As Brazil's cities have grown bigger, more modern, and more crowded, an indoor version of the game called *futsal* has become popular and allowed kids to sharpen their skills in gyms or indoor arenas. Private soccer academies have also grown more popular in Brazil, offering kids a way to devote themselves to and become better at the game.

There are many levels of amateur and professional teams across Brazil. The top league is the prestigious Brasileirão Serie A. Its twenty teams have national followings and long histories. Its players are regional and national heroes. The best of the best usually go on to play in Europe, home to the world's richest and most powerful leagues. Many European teams have scouts in Brazil watching for talented kids, and those clubs bring young players overseas to live and train in their own developmental academies.

Whatever the route, the more promise a player shows, the faster and farther he can rise through club ranks and ultimately reach the pros. After all, many Brazilians have gone from childhood poverty to world-superstar status because of their amazing soccer skills. Ronaldo and Ronaldinho are two recent examples of players who rose from Brazilian *favelas*, or slums, to earn million-dollar soccer salaries in Europe, win World Player of the Year awards, and lead the Brazilian national team to World Cup victory.

But beyond the huge salaries of pro players, Brazilian

*futebol* ignites a passion in its fans and players. Soccer is the national sport, and it is a big part of Brazil's national identity. It has won more World Cup championships than any other nation and shaped the game with its unique style.

There's a common saying about soccer: "England invented it. The Brazilians perfected it." The modern game of soccer was created in England in the 1830s, and it was a Scotsman who brought it to Brazil. A young man named Charles Miller brought two soccer balls home to Scotland with him after he completed his education in England. His father, like many British workers, moved to Brazil to work on the railroads, and Charles went with him. Charles began organizing soccer kickabouts in São Paulo that quickly caught on with the local people. Another Anglo-Brazilian, Oscar Cox, returned from school in Europe and brought the game to Rio de Janeiro. By 1900 the first soccer club was formed, and others followed soon after.

Slavery had only been ended in Brazil in 1888, so there was still much racism and social change taking place there at the turn of the century. The early soccer matches were originally reserved for British and European players of the upper class, but even the poor people noticed. The game was easy to copy—all that was required was a ball. So the former slaves and native Brazilians began playing their own games. They were first allowed to play at the top level when, in 1904, the Bangu Athletic Club in Rio decided to chose its players regardless of race. The more non-white players became incorporated into the clubs, the more Brazilian the game became.

The British version of the game was formal and regimented. But as Brazilians learned to play the game apart from the European-oriented clubs, they developed their own style that relied more on individual skill and movement.

A match in 1914 that pitted Exeter City from England against a team of Rio and São Paulo's finest players is considered the first Brazilian national team. Brazil won 2–0, and the people found a strong sense of national pride in the team.

That sense of pride and identity grew as Brazil evolved the sport. Brazil won its first World Cup in 1958, then followed with World Cup championships in 1962 and 1970. No other country had reached that mark in World Cup dominance, and the world hadn't seen the game played with the creative flair of Brazil and its standout star Pelé.

Pelé's fluid dribbling and ability to control the ball in ways that seemed impossible cemented his legacy as the greatest player ever. He was Brazil's ambassador to the world, and he was soccer's biggest ambassador, spreading the joy and development of the game around the globe, including to the United States when he finished his pro career there in the 1970s.

One aspect that sets soccer apart from other sports is its non-stopping clock. American football resets after each play. Basketball is filled with timeouts, and baseball pauses to switch offense and defense each inning. But soccer runs in one continuous flow with only a halftime break. The result is that every pass, touch, or possession of the ball has the ability to cause a ripple effect on the game as it keeps unfolding. It also gives soccer the ability to surge and flow like a symphony as teams battle to control the conductor's baton of momentum.

It's that graceful flow that has made soccer known as the beautiful game, and it was Pelé who epitomized Brazilian soccer and popularized the sport as *jogo bonita*, the beautiful game. Brazil plays with style and rhythm, flowing with quick unexpected passes, skillful dribbling and dodging, and graceful elegance while attacking the goal.

One nickname of the national team is the Samba Boys. The samba is the upbeat rhythmic music and dance played throughout Brazil. The Brazilians have made soccer look like a graceful dance set to its beat and a joyous celebration to be swept up in.

Soccer was as much a part of the culture Kaká grew up in as the Portuguese language he speaks. It is part of his heritage that shaped him as a player and a person.

### Pelé: The Greatest Ever

Born Edson Arantes do Nascimento, Pelé is considered the greatest soccer player of all time. His humble beginnings did not limit his ability, and he went from playing in the streets of Brazil with a "ball" made from a sock stuffed with newspapers to his first World Cup appearance in 1958 at the age of 17. During that World Cup he scored a hat trick (three goals) in the semifinal as well as two goals in the final, leading Brazil to its first World Cup Championship. He is the only player ever to win three World Cup trophies. Pelé spent most of his years playing for the São Paulo team, Santos, and became a national treasure in Brazil.

Pelé is known for his seemingly limitless and varied skills. He was not just an excellent attacker and scorer, he could do it all—dribbling, passing, and seeing the field in a way that few other players could. He was loved in Brazil and around the world.

He retired from club ball in 1971 but later came out of retirement to join the New York Cosmos. His style of play and love of the game gave soccer new life in the United Sates. His influence helped bring the World Cup to the United States in 1994 and played a role in the creation of Major League Soccer (MLS) in 1995.

Along with his spectacular performance as a player, Pelé served as Brazil's minister of sports and became a goodwill ambassador for UNICEF. In 1999 the Olympic Committee voted him Athlete of the Century.

# God and Soccer

Kaká's twelfth year was an important one for both his spiritual and soccer life, and the decisions he made then would guide him throughout the rest of his life.

Most Brazilians follow the Catholic tradition of faith and worship, but there have been many new Protestant churches growing in the country in the past few decades. Both of Kaká's parents are evangelical Christians. Their faith guided their home and family, and Kaká grew up with a great respect for faith in God.

"Little by little, I stopped simply hearing people talk about the Jesus my parents taught me. There came a time when I wanted to live my own experiences with God," he said when he was grown up.

When he was twelve he decided to be baptized. It was a meaningful experience that brought him closer to Jesus.

"When I was baptized in 1994, something supernatural happened to me," Kaká later told the British newspaper *Mail on Sunday*. "I cannot explain it, but after that experience I got closer to God; more in tune with him. At that moment I was really born spiritually. I began to know God more in-depth."

The young Christian also became more serious about his future in soccer that same year. He decided he wanted to become a professional and hoped to one day reach the top team at São Paulo FC. "If it doesn't work out as a player, I would certainly go into physical education," he would later tell *The Irish Times*.

His ball-handling abilities and keen knowledge of the game were his best skills and helped him to do well. But his small size kept him from standing out. He just wasn't strong enough physically. When he was twelve, he was the size of a ten-year-old because his bones weren't developing at a normal rate. He continued to lag behind his peers in growth. Kaká was used to being smaller, but it gave him opportunities to learn.

"It was hard, but I learned from it," Kaká later told the soccer magazine *442*. "I learned to fight for what I wanted and that was important."

Life was good at the São Paulo academy. Several hundred boys lived in the dorms there and shared Kaká's dreams. Many, like Marcelo Saragosa, had traveled from far away to pursue their soccer dreams. Marcelo was from the southern Brazilian state Santa Catarina. When he was twelve, his coach invited him to São Paulo for a tryout with the club. Of the two hundred other boys at the tryout, only Marcelo was chosen to stay.

The boys lived at the academy at dormitories similar to American college dorms. They did their schoolwork there and spent the rest of the time practicing soccer and training. Their favorite practices were the scrimmage games they played against each other. Kaká was known as a disciplined and hard working student and player. He often woke up two hours early to study so he could maintain his training and practice schedule.

On weekends most of the players would go home with their families. Marcelo's home was too far away, so one week Kaká asked, "Marcelo, do you want to spend Saturday and Sunday with me at my house?"

"Yeah, that would be great," Marcelo answered.

Soon Marcelo was spending every weekend with Kaká and his family in their comfortable São Paulo home. Kaká and Marcelo became best friends, and Marcelo grew to be another son and brother to the family. Mr. and Mrs. Leite would introduce him as "their other son from South Brazil," and kept Marcelo in line along with their own sons.

Marcelo attended church with the Leite family, and Kaká often prayed for Marcelo. Marcelo did not have a relationship with Jesus, but he would see Kaká reading his Bible often. The two friends talked about God and Kaká helped his friend begin a relationship with Jesus.

"He showed me some things that I need to change," Marcelo said. "He helped a lot with the Bible too."

The boys got involved in a Bible study through *Atletas*

Kaká poses for a picture with a São Paulo FC jersey, the club where he played from his childhood until his transfer to AC Milan, in 2003.

*de Cristo*, or Athletes for Christ, at the academy and learned more about God. It was an important time for them as they grew stronger in their faith.

"It makes me happy to read the Bible every day, to study it and to be in fellowship with God, and learn more and more about Jesus," Kaká would say as an adult. But he was gaining his love for God and his word even at a young age.

They also had lots of fun. One favorite activity of Kaká, Marcelo, and Digão was PlayStation. Of course, their favorite video game was soccer. Kaká and Digão would battle and battle with their digital teams. The boys also played during free time at the club. Kaká always chose AC Milan as his digital team, a foreshadowing of things to come.

## São Paulo Futebol Clube

São Paulo FC is the youngest of the major teams from the city and state of São Paulo, but it was still founded in 1930. The Tricolor struggled for a long time to earn themselves a place alongside the state's two traditional giants, Corinthians and Palmeiras.

But the club's motto—"Football is an art; we have another approach to the game"—helped them build a fan base. So did Artur Friedenreich, the team's legendary goal scorer who netted an incredible 1,329 goals in a twenty-six-year career. Friedenreich was the hero of the crowds packed into São Paulo stadium, known more commonly as Morumbi stadium. Officially, the arena holds 80,500 fans.

## Brazil's Diverse People

The people of Brazil are known for their consistently warm, friendly, expressive nature, and yet they are richly diverse and varied in ethnicity and culture. The Portuguese settlers who came during the colonization of Brazil were unlike settlers in many European colonies. Less concerned with conquest of a new land, many were convicts accused of crimes against religion or morality. The majority of them were men, and the resulting lack of Portuguese women meant that relationships and marriage with native Indian women (and later with female African slaves) were more common and accepted than in many other European colonies. During its history of slavery, around four million African slaves were transported to Brazil. That is seven times the number brought to the United States. This resulted in a very large black population—the largest outside of Africa. In fact, only Nigeria has a larger black population than Brazil.

Brazil's history of immigration continued with large numbers of immigrants continuing to come from Portugal, but many also coming from other nations including Germany, Italy, Japan, and the Middle East. The intense and widespread mixing of all these groups has formed a diverse population in Brazil. Almost all Brazilians have some combination of European, African, Native American, Asian, and Middle Eastern lineage. This variety of cultural backgrounds and traditions has brought some conflict to Brazil, but has also added color and flavor to the current culture.

Portuguese remains the dominant language of Brazil, but this mixing of peoples and cultures has influenced the language as well. The Indian and African dialects found throughout Brazil have impacted the development of Portuguese not only in Brazil, but around the world. As for religion, the Roman Catholic influence of Portugal has remained dominant, as roughly seventy-five percent of today's Brazilians belong to the Roman Catholic Church.

# The Accident

Kaká signed his first professional contract when he was fifteen. São Paulo welcomed him to its youth team, which is the same age range as Under–17 in the United States.

That year Kaká was five feet, three inches tall and weighed 110 pounds—still much smaller than the other players. The officials at São Paulo FC took him to see doctors in the city to see if they could stimulate his bone development. The doctors put Kaká on a special diet high in carbohydrates and creatine, a natural amino acid used to promote muscle growth.

Kaká's body began to respond, and he checked in with the doctors every three months. By the time he was seventeen he had reached five feet, nine inches but was still skinny. "I used to reassure his parents by saying, 'Don't worry, he'll grow. The rest of you are all tall,'" remembered Turibio Leite de Barros Neto, São Paulo's physical trainer.

Trainers continued to help him, and Kaká worked hard on a muscle building plan. In another year and a half he had added another twenty-two pounds to his frame, much of it muscle.

The teenager also had to deal with myopia, or nearsightedness. That meant he could see objects that were close, but people or objects far away were blurry. In decades past, it had been a national scandal when someone started a rumor that Pelé was nearsighted. But medical technology had advanced since then, and Kaká simply wore contact lenses to give him clear vision down the entire length of the soccer field. Later, as an adult, he had surgery to permanently give him perfect vision.

Kaká moved up to São Paulo's junior team, the equivalent of U–20 in the United States. His new size definitely helped him on the field to be able to out-muscle other players for the ball. However, he wasn't one of the eleven starting players and didn't get much opportunity to play in games for the juniors.

But the young midfielder took advantage of every opportunity to learn and grow as a player. He loved it when the junior team got to scrimmage against the pro team. And he had little patience for players who would dive, or take a fall on purpose, to try to get the referee to call a foul or award a penalty kick in their favor. He learned from every coach he had.

"The ones that didn't like me taught me perseverance, patience, how to fight for what I wanted," Kaká told *442* later in life. "From the ones that did pick me I learned about technique and tactics."

Overall Kaká's career was moving in the right direction, but it almost came to an end when he was eighteen in October 2000.

In the middle of the Paulista Junior Championship, Kaká received two yellow cards, so he was suspended from the following game. He took advantage of the break to visit his grandparents in Caldas Novas, a popular tourist area in central Brazil known for its hot water springs. While he was there, Kaká slid down a water slide headfirst and struck his head on the bottom of the pool. The impact twisted his neck. His brother asked him if he was okay and saw that Kaká's head was bleeding. He needed four stitches, and doctors took an x-ray. But everything seemed normal.

Kaká went home to São Paulo and practiced for two days, but the pain in his neck was unbearable. Doctors took more x-rays, which revealed a frightening diagnosis. Kaká had broken his neck. More precisely, he had fractured the sixth vertebra in the top of his spine. Doctors told the Leite family that their son was lucky not to be paralyzed and lucky to even be walking normally.

Back home the family thanked God for protecting Kaká. They began praying for healing and asking friends to pray as well. Kaká had to wear a neck brace and lay in bed for two months. But at the end of that time, he was completely healed.

"[The doctors] were talking about luck, and my family

was talking about God," Kaká later told *The Independent*. "We knew that it was his hand that had saved me."

The accident was a key point in Kaká's life, and one that shaped him permanently. Spiritually, it confirmed his faith and taught him that God was taking care of him. It was a difficult time that prompted Kaká to pray much more and trust God more deeply. Looking back on the event later in life, Kaká told Athletes in Action, "I do not think that it was a coincidence. I believe God had a purpose in that accident."

The recovery period also gave him a lot of time to think. Would he be able to play soccer again? If he did, what did he want his future to look like? What did he want to accomplish in life? As the athlete waited and considered what might happen, he made a list of ten goals:

1. Return to soccer
2. Become a professional
3. Become first string (one of the top twenty-five players)
4. Fight for a position in the top eighteen
5. Win a starting spot
6. Compete in the Under–20 World Cup
7. Be called to the adult national team
8. Play on the adult national team
9. Compete in the World Cup
10. Transfer to a big club in Italy or Germany

He returned to the game he loved, focused on accomplishing his new objectives. No one could have guessed how soon he would need a new list of goals.

## More Than One Way to Kick a Ball

Brazil is so obsessed with soccer that it has spilled over into the formation of many related games:

**Futsal:** Somewhat like a cross between soccer and ice hockey, futsal is incredibly popular in Brazil and around the world. In 2000, 160 countries applied to enter the World Championship. With five players to a side, this game is played on an indoor basketball court with a smaller ball and twenty-minute halves.

**Button football:** Soccer had barely been introduced to Brazil when kids started tearing buttons off their jackets to play a table-top version. They would flick their buttons at a small ball to try to get it into a miniature net. Today the game can be bought as a kit, and official buttons contain the names and faces of popular players.

**Beach soccer:** With so many Brazilians living near the beach, it is natural that they started playing their favorite sport on the sand. Beach football in Brazil peaked in the 1950s when there was still room on the uncrowded beaches to play. But today's beach soccer is a compact and high-scoring version that is still popular.

**Footvolley:** A combination of soccer and volleyball, this incredibly popular game is played on a beach volleyball court with two players on each side. The catch? Players can only use their feet, head, and chest.

## The Accident

**Footbull:** Played for fun at rodeos in rural areas of Brazil, spectators are chosen for two teams in the arena. Then a (relatively gentle) bull is released and the crowd is entertained watching the teams go for the ball, and the bull go for the teams.

# Instant *Craque*

Kaká's life was about to change dramatically.

Once he was healthy again, he returned to his role on the club: a hard-working reserve midfielder on the junior team who didn't see much playing time in games. One day, the coach of the Tricolor professional team, Vadão, asked the junior's coach for a midfielder and a forward to fill out his roster for a game the next day. The junior's coach pointed out Kaká.

"He doesn't play much because I have my starting eleven right now," the coach said. "But he's a good player."

Coach Vadão took his colleague's word and brought Kaká up to the pro team in early 2001. He played well in his professional game, even scoring a goal to help São Paulo defeat Santos 4–1.

March 7, 2001 was the day that Kaká went from promising young player to superstar. The game was the final of the Torneio Rio-São Paulo, or Rio-São Paulo Tournament, a yearly contest that determined the champion of the two major city's teams. São Paulo faced the powerful club Botafogo, but the game was held at the Tricolor's home stadium, the Morumbi, in front of 71,000 fans. The atmosphere was especially electric because São Paulo had never won this prestigious tournament.

Things didn't look good for the Tricolor, though, when Donizete of Botafogo scored in the thirty-ninth minute. The Fagão held the lead deep into the second half, and São Paulo's coach knew he needed to make some changes to have a chance at victory. He turned to his bench and brought Kaká into the game in the second half as a substitute for the future national star Luis Fabiano.

With ten minutes left in the game, a Paulista teammate played a high looping pass from midfield toward the right side of Botafogo's penalty box. Another player headed the ball back toward Kaká, who was on the center of the eighteen-yard line. He stuck out his right foot to receive the ball. It flipped behind the back of his defender. Kaká dodged a step to his left and the ball bounced once in front of him. The goalkeeper charged off his line. Kaká powered a shot low along the ground, beneath the diving goalie's outstretched arm and into the goal just inside the post.

"Gooooooal, Kaká of São Paulo!" the TV announcer shouted.

Kaká's teammates jumped all over him. Fans danced in the stands, and fireworks exploded over the Morumbi. São Paulo still had a chance.

Botafogo pressed hard to try to score a winning goal and had some dangerous opportunities. With eight minutes left, the Fagão had a dangerous free kick from the left wing just outside São Paulo's penalty box. Kaká ran across the field waving his arms to urge the crowd to cheer and chant louder. The kick sailed toward the goal but São Paulo's defense headed it away.

But Botafogo controlled the ball and attempted another shot from the eighteen-yard line. Stopped by the Paulista defense! And the counter attack was on. The São Paulo defender passed the ball forward and a midfielder raced with it up the right side of the field. He dribbled toward the middle of the field and sent a perfect curving pass to the left where Kaká came sprinting forward.

Kaká took two touches — left foot, right foot — and was inside Botafogo's penalty box. Three defenders had raced back, and now two were on him. He took a long step left, dragged his right foot for a split-second, almost hopping forward twice on his left foot. The defender lunged to his right as he faced Kaká. Suddenly Kaká tapped the ball back toward the center and pulled back his right foot to fire a low shot on goal. It rocketed inches above the grass between both defenders, just past the fingertips of the diving goalkeeper, and into the net.

"Goooooooal! For São Paulo!" the TV announcer shouted again. "Kaká! Shirt number thirty-three! His second goal turns the game!"

Teammates buried Kaká under a jumping huddle. Fans embraced in the stands, and the coach pumped both fists in the air. More fireworks lit the night sky overhead.

Eight minutes later the referee blew the final whistle. São Paulo had won! In less than two minutes, Kaká had scored two goals to secure victory and bring the elusive championship to São Paulo.

Kaká raised both hands above his head and pointed toward the sky. Teammates embraced their new hero. Fans waved sparklers and shot off their own firecrackers in the stands. As the Tricolor celebrated, reporters swarmed around Kaká.

Kaká in action during the São Paulo and Guarani Paulista championship match, March 25, 2001.

"Kaká, two goals, eighteen years old. It's got to be emotional," a reporter said, thrusting a microphone in Kaká's face.

"It's very emotional," the new hero replied. "God is faithful. I'm not saying that God made the goals, but he gave me the opportunity."

The eighteen-year-old's life would never be the same. He was now a *craque*, the Portuguese word for ace.

## São Paulo FC Titles

The São Paulo Football Club is one of the most successful club teams in Brazil, holding the most national league and international titles of any Brazilian club. Their championships include:

FIFA Club World Cup: 2005

Intercontinental Cup: 1992, 1993

Libertadores Cup: 1992, 1993, 2005

Campeonato Brasileiro Série A: 1977, 1986, 1991, 2006, 2007, 2008

Copa Sudamericana: 2012

# Sudden Fame

Overnight everyone knew who Kaká was. Before the Rio-São Paulo tournament, he lived a normal life and could go anywhere without being recognized. Not anymore.

Two weeks after his breakout game, he and Marcelo went to a shopping mall. "Hey, Kaká!" someone shouted. Quickly there were about a hundred people clamoring around and pushing to get close to their new star. "Kaká! Kaká!" they shouted, trying to get autographs and meet him. Kaká and Marcelo couldn't even walk. They had to have help from the security guards to be able to leave.

Interestingly, before the Rio-São Paulo Tournament the team and media had been spelling his name with c's, Caca. The player had asked them before to change it, but nothing had been done. Now that his name was on the whole city's lips, both quickly corrected the spelling to Kaká.

Girls especially loved the young soccer star. After all, he was young and good-looking. The girls formed fan clubs and Web sites and posted pictures of their favorite player. They wanted to know everything about him, especially whether or not he had a girlfriend! They also mailed gifts and wrote letters expressing their admiration and love. Kaká began receiving fifty letters each day. His mother tried to answer them all, but the numbers were simply too much.

The media wanted as much of Kaká as possible too, and his face began to appear on many magazine covers, from sports publications to *Istoé Gente*, Brazil's edition of *People* magazine. It took some getting used to, and Kaká seemed shy at first. But he got plenty of practice and quickly got used to speaking to reporters and the media.

Brazil loves its celebrities, especially its futebol stars, so Kaká and his family weren't completely taken by surprise. What was surprising was how quickly it came. Still, Kaká remained humble and gracious about all the attention and expressed appreciation for his fans' support when he spoke to the press about it. He looked at his new fame and success as a blessing from God and a platform that would allow him to share God's love with many people.

Kaká's family also supported him and helped him deal with all the new attention. He maintained the same lifestyle he always had and didn't let his fame change his attitude or outlook. He always wore a bracelet that read

*Jesus*, and his trademark celebration became pointing to the sky with both arms upraised to give thanks to God. He also remained loyal to his friends.

One friend and fellow player, Maldonado, told *Istoé Gente* magazine that Kaká hadn't changed, even with all his achievements. "Kaká is a good friend who I can talk to about anything," he said.

One thing Kaká didn't talk about, though, was girls— even to his best friend Marcelo. He was simply too focused on soccer. "In order for me to have a girlfriend, it would have to be a fundamental point in my life," he told *Istoé Gente*. "I can't be thinking of her when I should be concentrating and preoccupied with the game."

He avoided girls who only wanted to get close to him because he was a famous soccer player by avoiding dance clubs and wild parties. Instead, he preferred to hang out with his family or friends, and he only dated girls who were already friends or were friends of his friends.

On the field, Kaká's heroic performance against Botafogo had earned him a starting position for São Paulo, and he made the most of it. He scored twelve goals in twenty-seven games during his rookie season.

Sports writers and fans compared him to great Brazilian players, such as Leonardo, Raí, and Socrates. Kaká was honored. Raí had been his favorite player growing up, and Kaká had even followed the São Paulo great into the locker room to ask for an autograph once! But Kaká remained focused on his own game.

"They say I look like Raí and that's an honor. He's an excellent man and a great player," Kaká told *Veja* magazine. "At the beginning everyone searched for references, but that will slowly pass until I make my own mark as Kaká."

Unbelievably, Kaká had achieved the first eight of his ten goals fifteen months after his life-threatening accident that should have ended his career. But the final two were the biggest of all: the World Cup and the European leagues. Some players worked for years and never made the national team or the world's top leagues.

## Raí

Kaká often names the Brazilian player Raí as one of his biggest influences. Raí Souza Vieira de Oliveira was born on May 15, 1965. He played club football in Brazil, including for São Paulo from 1987–1993. He then left Brazil and played for Paris St. Germain for five years before returning to São Paulo in 1998 for the end of his career, retiring in 2000.

Raí was a midfielder and, while he didn't make a huge impact on the international soccer scene, he was arguably São Paulo FC's best player of all time, having won every kind of championship for the team during his time there.

"I admired him because he was the top player at São Paulo when I was starting out," says Kaká. "He was a leader who decided games and he was the big name. He was an elegant player and very talented, and that impressed me."

## Zico

---

Another of Kaká's favorite players was Zico, the Brazilian soccer sensation of the time when Kaká was young. Zico is considered one of the best midfielders the world has ever seen. Born Arthur Antunes Coimbra in 1953 in Rio de Janeiro, Brazil, Zico played for the Brazilian national team in the 1978, 1982, and 1986 World Cups. Brazil didn't win any of those championships, even though the 1982 team was one of their strongest national teams ever. He played the bulk of his professional career for the Brazilian club Flamengo, but also spent a few years in Italy and Japan. He also went on to coach in Japan, including the Japanese national team in the 2006 World Cup. On the field, Zico made seemingly impossible goals in all imaginable ways. He was a free kick specialist and playmaking midfielder with excellent vision of the field. As a result, he also dished out many assists.

# The Yellow and Green

Kaká caught the eye of more than the Brazilian girls. European scouts took note of this young player and began to consider his potential role on their teams. But perhaps the most important head to turn Kaká's way was that of Luiz Felipe Scolari, the head coach of Brazil's national team.

Coach Scolari called Kaká to train with the *Seleção*, or Selection, as Brazilians call their national team. On January 31, 2002, Kaká pulled on the famous yellow and green jersey of his country for the first time. The match was a friendly against Bolivia. That meant the game didn't count toward any qualification or placement for the World Cup, but both sides wanted to win. It was basically a scrimmage with international pride on the line, and a chance for players like Kaká to gain experience and test their mettle against other nations.

For Kaká it was a momentous occasion. He told his friend, Marcelo, that when he put the national jersey on, everything changed. "For a soccer player, there is no more beautiful thing to do," Marcelo recalled later.

Brazil defeated Bolivia 6–0, and Kaká played the second half. He didn't score, but he did make a positive impression on Scolari. The coach called upon him for another match against Iceland in March. This time he started the game and played all ninety minutes. He even scored his first goal for Brazil's national team in the forty-seventh minute to help Brazil claim a decisive 6–1 victory.

On May 23, Kaká went to the São Paulo training center to get treatment for an ankle injury. He told his parents he would be gone all day, but he returned early in the afternoon to surprise his parents. They turned on the TV to watch Coach Scolari announcing the twenty-three players who would be on the roster for the World Cup. There was no surprise about Brazil's national stars such as Ronaldo, Ronaldinho, Rivaldo, and Cafu. But when Coach Scolari announced the twenty-third and final player on the squad, joyous celebration broke out. "Kaká of São Paulo," he told the nation. Kaká was going to the World Cup in South Korea and Japan.

Brazilians were worried about their team heading into the world's greatest soccer competition. Expectations were always sky-high for the Seleção, partly because their team had built such an astonishing record of international dominance. At that point, Brazil had won four World Cup championships, more than any other nation.

Kaká controls the ball during a friendly football game against FC Luzern Selection, in preparation for the 2006 World Cup, May 30, 2006, in Basel, Switzerland.

Fabrice Coffrini/AFP/Getty Images

Even more, in its twelve previous World Cup qualifying campaigns combined, they had only lost one match.

This time the Brazilians had lost six games in reaching the World Cup, and they barely qualified at all. It took a victory over Venezuela in the final match to secure the fourth and final qualifying spot from South America. Even Ecuador placed higher, a team that had never before qualified for a World Cup. The Golden Squad appeared tarnished heading to the world's grandest tournament.

To make matters worse for fans, the previous 1998 World Cup in France had been viewed as a huge disappointment. Brazil had been viewed as a favorite to win. They reached the final game but were destroyed 3–0 by the host team.

Superstar Ronaldo had experienced a mysterious illness before the match, and it became part of the focus of government hearings and investigations into the national soccer federation. Brazil's top levels of soccer organization experienced upheaval and chaos, and the nation demanded more from their Seleção.

"It's a big responsibility to play on the Brazil team because as everyone knows, when it's time for the World Cup, the players on the team become more important than the president," said defender Edmilson.

"From the moment you become a professional, you have to learn to deal with the pressures and the fact that in football, Brazil is always favorite," Ze Roberto added in *The Prize*.

This was the difficult climate Kaká was heading into, but nothing could dampen his elation over being chosen for the team heading to the first World Cup to be hosted in Asia. One bizarre event had helped him make the squad: another talented attacking midfielder named Djalminha who was seen as competition for Kaká's spot on the roster had gotten mad and headbutted Coach Scolari during training. While he admitted the event had influenced his decision, Scolari insisted that Kaká's performance had made the real difference.

Kaká was seen as the baby of the team. He was the younger brother in the Family Scolari, the up-and-comer brought along for experience, just as Ronaldo had been in 1994 and Ronaldinho in 1998. That shared experience helped Kaká and Ronaldinho bond instantly, and Kaká looked to the outgoing superstar to help him learn the ropes of this new level. "Everything that I needed, I asked him—including what type of toothpaste to use," Kaká later told *Istoé Gente*.

Maybe he would pick up some goal-scoring tips from the Brazilian phenomenon as well.

### One Team, Many Names

Just as Brazilian players are known by their nicknames, so is its national team. The most common name is *A Seleção* which means "the Selection." But *seleção* is also the Portuguese term used for any team from any country, so it's not unusual for Brazilians to distinguish the national team with the names *Seleção Brasileira* or, more specifically, *A Seleção Brasileira de Futebol*.

The team is also commonly called *O Canarinho*, which means "the Little Canary." This name has been around since the 1950 World Cup when it was popularized by a cartoonist named Fernando Pierucutti.

Other nicknames for Brazil's team include *Pentacampeões* (Five-time champions), the *Canarinhos* (Canaries), *Verdeamarelos* (Green and Yellows) or the *Auriverdes* (Green

# The Yellow and Green

and Golds) — the latter three inspired by the national flag and team colors. Other names, such as the Samba Boys or Samba Kings, have come from other news media in other countries.

## Brazil's World Cup Leaders

Three players from Brazil have appeared in four World Cup tournaments each. They are led only by Lothar Matthäus of Germany and Antonio Carbajal of Mexico, who have each played in five World Cups. The leading Brazilians are:

Pelé (1958, '62, '66, '70)

Djalma Santos (1954, '58, '62, '66)

Cafu (1994, '98, '02, '06)

# World Champion

Brazil opened the World Cup with a 2–1 victory over Turkey and never looked back. Ronaldo did the same, scoring against Turkey and going on to be the tournament's highest scorer with eight goals overall. Brazilians were relieved to see their beloved hero finding the net.

In the Canarinho's third and final game of the opening round, Brazil held a solid lead over Costa Rica. Coach Scolari turned to his bench and sent Kaká into the game for the final twenty-five minutes. The rookie played well, and Brazil won 5–2, securing first place in its group and advancing to the knockout rounds.

Next up for Brazil was Belgium. A controversial call cancelled a Belgian goal that would have given them a 1–0 lead, but Brazil ended up winning 2–0. The quarter-finals brought an always charged Brazil versus England match — the game's inventors against its perfecters.

England claimed the lead in the twenty-third minute on a Michael Owen goal, giving Brits hope that their country could regain soccer supremacy. But at forty-five minutes, Rivaldo equalized just before halftime. Ronaldinho struck quickly in the second half. He sent a screaming free kick that kissed the bottom of the crossbar and landed in the net as the English's goalkeeper David Seaman watched flatfooted. But Ronaldinho later received a harsh red card that sent him out of the game, and Brazil had to play with only ten men for the game's final thirty-two minutes. They still held on to win and advance.

The semifinal game was a rematch of Brazil's first game against Turkey, and once again the yellow and green prevailed. This time Ronaldo scored his sixth goal of the tournament to deliver a 1–0 victory.

Meanwhile, on the other side of the bracket, Germany relied on a single goal by Michael Ballack and stellar goalkeeping by Oliver Kahn to down two hot under-dogs: the United States in the quarterfinals and hosts Korea Republic in the semis. However, Ballack's second booking with a yellow card against Korea meant that Germany's star would have to sit out of the final.

The table was set for a duel of soccer superpowers: Brazil and Germany on June 30, 2002. Germany was expected to hang back and rely on its defense, but the Germans came out attacking and looking like the more dangerous team in the first half. Brazil still had scoring chances but even Ronaldo couldn't convert them. He blew two golden opportunities in the first half. As the first half wound down, teammate Kleberson struck the German crossbar and goalkeeper Kahn came up with a huge save of a Ronaldo blast. The game remained a scoreless tie at halftime.

Germany kept up the attack again in the second half, and a Jens Jeremies' header was blocked on the goal line by Brazilian defender Edmilson. The Brazilian keeper Marcos was also forced to deflect a thundering thirty-yard German free kick off his post to keep it out of the net. The battle continued.

Then Ronaldo caught fire midway through the second half. Rivaldo fired a shot on goal in the sixty-seventh minute. It appeared that the goalie Kahn should have caught it, but he could only deflect it. Ronaldo pounced on the rebound and sent the ball into the net past the diving Kahn. Twelve minutes later Ronaldo slotted the ball past Kahn again, giving Brazil a 2–0 lead that they would not surrender.

As the game's final minutes ticked away, Coach Scolari told Kaká to warm up on the sidelines. He was going in the game. The twenty-year-old stood on the sideline of the World Cup final, waiting to set foot on the pitch as the referee blew his final whistle. There was never a break in the play to let him in the game. Still, Kaká was a world champion.

The Brazilian sideline erupted into wild celebration. Kaká ran onto the field directly to teammates Edmilson and Lucio. The three immediately fell to their knees, clasped hands, and prayed. "I believe that the emotions ran high, but the important part for us was to kneel and give glory to God," Lucio later said on *The Prize*.

Once they had thanked God, they got up and embraced. The Christian teammates wore white t-shirts with different messages about God. Kaká's read "I belong to Jesus." Edmilson's said "Jesus loves you" and Lucio's "God is faithful." They waved to fans and celebrated with the rest of the team. Kaká draped a Brazilian flag around his shoulders. Many of the players wept with joy.

If playing in the World Cup was another goal accomplished for Kaká, holding the trophy aloft as World Cup champion was a dream come true. Team captain Cafu lifted the golden cup first, and the entire nation of Brazil rejoiced. "It's a fantastic feeling to be a Brazilian tonight," Ronaldo said after the match.

It was many people's favorite moment when the tearful Ronaldo raised the cup, but Kaká will never forget when the superstar striker handed the cup to Kakito, as Ronaldo called him. Back in the locker room, the entire squad joined hands and knelt in a circle to pray and thank God for their victory. All of this was only the beginning of the celebration.

"To get to the World Cup at twenty, to be with the great players, was amazing," Kaká later said to London's *Daily Mail.* "You learn a lot from the players — to create, to keep trying even if you make a mistake, because at some point you will get it right. And you lose a bit of fear. You realize that, although the players are extraordinary, they are normal people."

It was invaluable experience that Kaká hoped to be able to put to good use later.

## World Cup Awards

Every team's goal at the World Cup is to win the championship. But there are other honors given out to teams and individual players. These six awards are also presented at the end of the World Cup:

*The Golden Ball:* Presented to the most outstanding player as decided by a vote of media members. The Silver Ball and the Bronze Ball are also given to the players finishing second and third in the voting.

*The Golden Shoe:* This award is sometimes called the Golden Boot, and is given to the tournament's top goal scorer. Recently, Silver and Bronze shoe awards have been awarded to the second and third top goal scorers as well.

*The Yashin Award:* Given to the best goalkeeper, decided by the FIFA Technical Study Group.

*The Best Young Player Award:* Given to the best player who is 21 years old or younger at the start of the calendar year. This award is also decided by the FIFA Technical Study Group.

*The FIFA Fair Play Trophy:* The team with the best record of fair play is handed this award. It is decided by a points system and criteria established by the FIFA Fair Play Committee.

*The Most Entertaining Team:* The general public gets to vote on the team that has been most entertaining for fans.

## The World Cup Trophy

Stolen twice, protected from the Nazis, sold at auction, accidentally broken, and recreated—the World Cup trophies have lived an exciting life.

## World Champion

• There have been two official trophies since the World Cup began in 1930. The first was called *Victory,* and later renamed *The Jules Rimet* trophy in honor of the former FIFA president. The second is the FIFA World Cup trophy still in use today.

• The *Victory* trophy was held in Italy during World War II. Fearing the cup would not be safe at the bank in Rome, the Italian Vice President hid it in a shoebox under his bed to keep Nazis from taking it.

• Four months before the 1966 World Cup, the trophy was stolen from an exhibition. It was found wrapped in newspaper at the bottom of a suburban garden hedge in South London by a dog named Pickles.

• In light of security issues, a secret replica was made and used in post-match celebrations. That replica was bought by FIFA at an auction in 1997 for such a high price that some speculate the trophy being sold wasn't the replica, but the genuine cup.

• In line with the original rules, Brazil got to keep the trophy permanently in 1970 with their third World Cup win. But they didn't keep it for long—it was stolen again in 1983 from a display at the Brazilian Football Confederation in Rio de Janeiro. The trophy was never recovered and the investigation concluded it was melted down for its gold. A replacement was commissioned and presented in Brazil in 1984.

• In need of a new cup for 1974, FIFA commissioned artist Silvio Gazzaniga. The new creation was gold with two layers of malachite, a green stone. Unlike the previous trophy, this one is the permanent property of FIFA, and each winning team has its name engraved on the name plate on the bottom of the trophy.

• Italy won the Cup in 2006. Just days after their win, it was reported that a piece of green malachite had broken off and was glued back on.

What will the future hold for the trophy? Stay tuned. It's not easy being the World Cup.

# Europe Calling

The Seleção were national heroes. Their 2002 World Cup championship was the nation's fifth. Brazil had now won a World Cup on all five of the continents that had hosted the event.

As their chartered Varig Airlines jet flew home, it was met by military jets to provide an escort for the final few miles. The team jet had its fuselage painted with the players' faces, and it circled over the capital, Brasília, so the whole city could salute the team.

After landing, Cafu came through the plane's door first and held the World Cup trophy over his head. The city, dressed in bright yellow and green, went wild. Fireworks exploded. An Air Force band struck up a samba beat, and the party was on.

Next came the parade to the presidential palace. The players loaded onto two trucks, and it took them four hours to drive the nine miles past several hundred thousand screaming fans.

Brazilians love their futebol team, and they love to celebrate. Life is even better when the two come together.

Expectations were high for Kaká back at São Paulo, and the attacking midfielder continued his winning ways during the 2002 season. He scored ten goals in twenty-two games that year and won the Bola de Ouro, or Golden Ball. The award is given to the best player of the Brazilian League. The Tricolor also came close to winning Brazil's national championship, finishing the regular season in first place but losing in the playoffs. Even though the Paulistas didn't win the championship, Kaká was awarded the tournament's Golden Ball award for the best player.

Much of São Paulo's success was due to Kaká, and São Paulo rewarded him with a $20 million contract. Instead of rushing out to buy a fancy car, Kaká used his money to help pay his brother Digão's college tuition.

Early in 2002, Kaká had met a beautiful girl named Caroline Celico. She had long dark hair and brown eyes. Mr. Leite knew her mother, who was the director of the international fashion design company Dior in Brazil. Their parents introduced them, and Kaká and Caroline exchanged phone numbers.

Kaká went to see Caroline for her fifteenth birthday and began to get to know her. She was younger than the nineteen-year-old Kaká, but that didn't bother him.

His only concern was that she didn't share his Christian faith — yet.

The two began dating after Kaká returned from the World Cup. He took her to church and told her about his relationship with Jesus, and soon she too entrusted her life to Christ. The couple fell in love and began dreaming of marriage. But Caroline was still in school, and they would have to wait several years before they could marry. There would be challenges along the way.

There were also challenges coming for Kaká on the soccer field. Other teams knew that he was São Paulo's leader and playmaker, so they put their best defenders on Kaká to try to shut down the Tricolor attack. Kaká's schedule became extra busy as he also played internationally for the Brazilian Under–23 team. And he also had to deal with an injury, a muscle tear that needed to heal.

Fans continued to mob Kaká in public, and their expectations grew. They wanted a championship, and they wanted it soon. Kaká's goal-scoring dropped off early in the season, and some fans began to boo him on the field. Some criticized him, saying he was too focused on moving to a European team. Several clubs there had expressed interests, and Kaká's agent was negotiating with them and São Paulo FC about money and contractual terms.

Kaká handled all the pressure with his usual grace, saying that it was good preparation for being a player on a national championship-caliber team or one who could make it in the top European leagues.

Kaká shows the scarf of his new team, AC Milan, as he arrives at the San Siro stadium in Milan, Italy, prior to the start of the "Luigi Berlusconi trophy" exhibition soccer match between AC Milan and Juventus, August 17, 2003.

Manchester United, the world-famous powerhouse from the English Premier League, showed interest in bringing Kaká to its club. German giant Bayer Leverkusen of the Bundesliga offered about 15 million euros, and Brescia of the Italian Serie A offered around 12.5 million. CSKA Moscow in Russia was also interested. But Kaká had his heart on one team, and they were in the running too. AC Milan had always been his favorite. Plus the former Brazil and São Paulo player Leonardo was an executive with Milan, and he was eager to bring Kaká to Italy.

Kaká celebrating with a T-shirt reading "I belong to Jesus" after AC Milan beat Liverpool in the UEFA Champions League Final on May 23, 2007.

© Sampics/Corbis

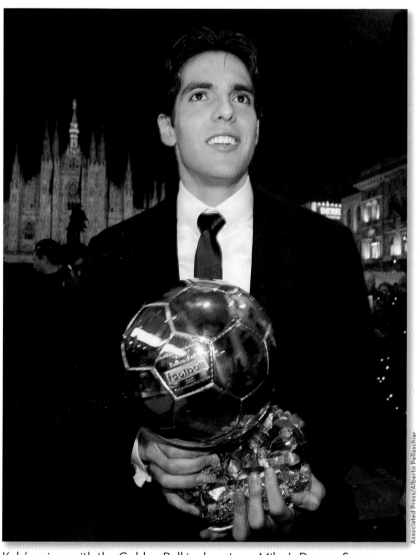

Kaká arrives with the Golden Ball in downtown Milan's Duomo Square, Sunday, December 2, 2007. Kaká won the Golden Ball award after helping the Italian club win the Champions League title this year with some standout performances. The young Brazil international scored 10 goals in the competition with his two-goal performance at Manchester United in the semifinals being hailed as one of the best of the tournament.

Real Madrid's Kaká kicks the ball during a Spanish La Liga soccer match against Racing Santander at the Santiago Bernabeu stadium in Madrid, Saturday, November 21, 2009.

Kaká works out during AC Milan's practice session for the Club World Cup soccer championship in Yokohama, near Tokyo, Japan, Monday, December 10, 2007. Kaká always works hard at practice and continues pushing himself to improve his skills.

Kaká kicks the ball during his team's practice session for the Club World Cup soccer championship at Yokohama International Stadium in Yokohama, near Tokyo, Wednesday, December 12, 2007.

Kaká shoots during the Champions League soccer match against Zurich at the Santiago Bernabeu stadium in Madrid, on Wednesday, November 25, 2009.

Kaká is tackled by Eyong Enoh of AFC Ajax during the UEFA Champions League Group D match between Real Madrid and AFC Ajax at Estadio Santiago Bernabeu on September 27, 2011 in Madrid, Spain.

Kaká, right, and Heerenveen's Mika Vayrynen, vie for the ball during their UEFA Cup group E soccer match at Abe Lenstra stadium in Heerenveen, northern Netherlands, Thursday, October 23, 2008.

Real Madrid's new player Kaká from Brazil reacts, during a press conference after his presentation at the Santiago Bernabeu stadium in Madrid, Tuesday, June 30, 2009. Kaká ushered in Real Madrid's latest 'galactico' era as the Spanish club gave the Brazil player a rock star welcome with an unveiling in front of at least 50,000 fans.

A deal was reached. In July 2003, Kaká was headed for Italy to be a part of Milan's Rossoneri, or Red-Blacks. He would be paid 8.5 million Euros, about 10.6 million U.S. dollars at the time.

The tenth and final goal from Kaká's list was accomplished in only two and a half years. It was time to set his sights on new challenges. Finding challenges wouldn't be any trouble in the excellent Italian league.

### The Brazilian Pro League

The highest division of Brazilian football is called Campeonato Brasileirão da Série A. It is often referred to as simply Brasileirão. Twenty teams qualify for this division each year, and Flamengo and São Paulo have dominated competition since this national league began in 1971.

### In and Out of the League

Promotion and relegation is a system used by sports leagues worldwide, especially in European football leagues. At the end of each season, teams are transferred between divisions according to their ranking. The best-ranked teams from a lower division are promoted to the next-highest division, while the lowest-ranked teams in a higher division are relegated to the lower division. In Brasileirão, four teams are relegated each year and replaced by four teams being promoted, to make up the new list of twenty.

# Benvenuti in Italia

Kaká was a bit of a mystery arriving in Italy. When it comes to club teams and national leagues, Europe is the center of the football universe. The biggest players, teams, and leagues exist there—along with the biggest money and power. Because the countries are close together geographically and their teams compete against each other in Union of European Football Associations (UEFA) leagues, many fans know about the players in other countries. Brazil is known and respected worldwide, but the average European soccer fan doesn't necessarily follow Brazil's up and comers—until they head to Europe, that is.

European soccer is generally considered more physical and tactical than South American soccer. South American soccer has a reputation for being more stylistic and free-flowing. It is not uncommon for South

American players to struggle with the adjustment to Europe at first, and Milan's coach Carlo Ancelotti wanted to give his new twenty-one-year-old import time to settle into his new club and continent. He and the team's leaders expected Kaká to spend his first year learning and developing while coming off the bench a little bit to get some game experience in Italy.

Besides, Milan already had a star midfielder in Manuel Rui Costa, a Portuguese legend. They also had Kaká's Seleção teammate Rivaldo, another midfielder. Kaká was willing to learn but also committed to contributing as much as he could to his new team.

"I knew that I had to adapt to European football," he later told England's *The Times*. "I am just one man, I knew it wasn't going to adapt to me. At the same time, I knew that if they signed me it was because I could provide something different."

That something different was Kaká's blend of skillful style and physical strength. By now he was six feet, one inch, weighed about 180 pounds, and had fully grown into his body.

Former Brazilian national team coach Vanderlei Luxemburgo said, "Kaká has the technique of a Brazilian and the physical qualities of a European. He is the standard-bearer of the modern game."

The question was, how long would he take to be able to fully show it?

Kaká's answer: immediately. He wasted no time in making a big impression on his new coaches, teammates, and fans. Within his first week he scored his first goal in a preseason match against Genoa. In about a month he had earned a starting spot for the 2003–2004 season, pushing Rui Costa to the bench. When asked how he felt about it, Rui Costa answered, "He is simply extraordinary."

Kaká usually played at the top of Milan's five-man midfield behind Ukrainian striker Andriy Shevchenko or Clarence Seedorf. Either way, it was a lethal combination. Kaká's vision of the field and understanding of where the game and its players were heading were exceptional. The Rossoneri wanted to get the ball to their midfielder, because he was able to move it up the field and deliver it at the feet of the goal-scoring specialists. But even while feeding passes to Milan's strikers, Kaká managed to score ten goals of his own in his first season.

Milan found itself in a heated three-way battle for first place in Serie A with Juventus and Roma. By December it appeared that the Rossoneri would be out of contention, but on January 6, Kaká's assist to Shevchenko enabled the winning goal over Roma that put Milan back on top. Kaká also contributed with a goal and assist against Inter Milan and an assist against Roma that gave Milan key victories. Milan won the Scudetto, the Serie A title, and Kaká was named the Player of the Year.

Naturally Milan's fans loved their new hero, which helped to make Kaká's transition to a new country easier. It wasn't too big a leap. The Italians are generally warm and expressive, much like Brazilians. And Milan has many similarities to São Paulo. Located in Northern Italy, it is the nation's largest city. Like São Paulo, it is a business and cultural center. It's also an international fashion capital. The stylish Kaká fit in well, as he was already a model and representative for the designer Giorgio Armani.

Kaká loved the delicious Italian food, as well. What was hard was being far away from his family and Caroline. While paparazzi looked for every opportunity to snap photos of the Brazilian celebrity, Kaká avoided them and the temptations of aggressive female fans by staying away from Milan's nightlife. He kept the same quiet lifestyle as he had back in Brazil, and didn't visit Milan's famous dance clubs.

Being 6,300 miles away from Caroline was difficult, but life for Kaká was off to an excellent start in Italy. AC Milan's president, Silvio Berlusconi, who also happens to be the Prime Minister of Italy, laughed and said, "It looks like the boy has a few good qualities, no?" He also said that Kaká was far more valuable than every million they had paid to get him, calling the 8.5 million Euros "peanuts."

Kaká took it all with humility. "He's a well-balanced, laid-back young man, who is not prone to either over-excitement or depression," coach Ancelotti said. "He is mentally very strong and already very mature beyond his years. I don't think there's much risk of him getting bigheaded. He is a great champion."

## San Siro Stadium

Home to both AC Milan and Internazionale, San Siro is a stadium icon in the world of soccer. It is officially named Stadio Giuseppe Meazza in honor of the player for Internazionale and AC Milan in the 1930s and 1940s. He was also a two-time World Cup winner. The stadium is more commonly called San Siro because of its location in the San Siro district of Western Milan. It underwent major renovations for the 1990 World Cup and currently seats almost 86,000. A museum located inside the stadium commemorates the history and achievements of both teams.

## Learning the Hard Way

Opponents only thought they were ready for Kaká the next season. Opposing coaches studied the twenty-two-year-old's moves and tendencies and sent their best defenders to slow him down.

It made a difference, and Kaká was slowed down somewhat. Some media and experts criticized him for not being able to keep up the phenomenal pace of his first year, but Kaká knew he was young and still had plenty to learn.

"It has been more difficult than last year," Kaká said. "I am known in Italy now. The markers know me, and they are tough here."

To adjust, Coach Ancelotti gave his playmaker more freedom to move wider on the wings. It gave him more room to escape from his markers, or it pulled his defenders wide, opening up more room in the middle for teammates to do their damage.

Kaká didn't score as many goals in 2005–2006, but he still finished with seven in thirty-six games. And he continued to become the leader of his team.

What some have called his greatest goal at Milan came in September at San Siro during an important EUFA Champions League match against Turkey's Fenerbahce. Kaká had scored the Rossoneri's first goal in the eighteenth minute on a low, twenty-four-yard drive just inside the post. But with the game tied 1–1 and less than five minutes to play, Kaká received the ball on the left wing. On a full-speed run, he shook off one defender and dodged another as he ducked toward the middle of the field. With a little open space, he blurred past another defender at the top of the box. It appeared they were standing still as the red and black of Kaká's number twenty-two jersey blew by. Now there was only the goalkeeper in his way. He took one more touch on the ball, then blasted a right-footed shot along the ground, below the goalie's lunge, and inside the near post. Goal!

The TV announcers compared the display to the legendary Argentine Diego Maradona. Such praise was becoming commonplace for the young Brazilian.

"Someone with Kaká's talent and qualities comes along only once every fifty years," said Carlos Alberto Parreira, Brazil's new national coach. "He is the future example for every player in the Brazil team."

Even the great Pelé, widely considered the best to ever play the game, agreed. "In Brazil, we have very good players in all positions, but I think the outstanding talent at the moment is Kaká," Pele said. "He is very skillful and already one of the best players in the world."

What dazzled most was Kaká's efficiency and elegance. His moves were not flashy and jittery-quick; instead, he attacked directly and glided by defenders, controlling the ball seemingly effortlessly at full speed. None of his motions was wasted. "He will always try to go vertically rather than horizontally," his coach Ancelotti said. "He will never take the extra, unnecessary touch."

Perhaps what made him most dangerous of all was Kaká's work ethic. He always practiced and played hard, and he continued to listen to and learn from his coaches.

Kaká's favorite highlight came early in 2005. First he called Caroline's father from Milan and asked for permission to marry her. Then he took his sweetheart to Venice, the romantic Italian city where the streets are watery canals, and boatmen sing as they row their gondolas.

At dinner Kaká offered her a beautiful ring and asked her to be his wife. She said yes, and the couple began planning to marry later that year.

Back on the field, a storybook soccer ending seemed to be lining up as well. All across Europe, the top teams from each league play games in a season-long tournament arranged by UEFA. The best of the best compete in the Champions League, first in round-robin play, then in best-of-two-game elimination rounds. The ultimate winner of a single final game is crowned the best team in Europe and is generally considered the best team in the world.

AC Milan had reached the finals of the Champions League and would face the English team Liverpool in the finals. The match couldn't have begun better for Milan. Captain Paolo Maldini volleyed in a shot within the first minute to give the Rossoneri an immediate lead. Liverpool came close on several scoring chances but Milan's keeper Dida came up with the saves. In the thirty-eighth minute, Kaká dribbled into Liverpool's side and passed the ball to Andriy Shevchenko, who passed to Hernán Crespo on the far post. Crespo buried a shot in the net: 2–0 Milan. Crespo struck again a minute before halftime, taking a pass from Kaká and chipping over Liverpool's goalie Jerzy Dudek.

With a three-goal lead at the half, Milan seemed to have the championship in hand, but Liverpool refused to surrender. The Reds shifted their lineup around and went on a desperate attack. Their efforts paid off quickly as captain Steven Gerrard headed in a cross from John Arne Riise nine minutes into the half. Liverpool was on the scoreboard. Vladimír Šmicer added another goal two minutes later, and the momentum was fully in Liverpool's favor.

Less than four minutes after that, Liverpool was awarded a penalty kick when Milan defender Gennaro Gattuso fouled Gerrard in the box. Xabi Alonso lined up the ball on the twelve-yard penalty stripe and faced off against goalkeeper Dida. The kick came low for the left post. Dida dove. Save! But the live ball rebounded out and Alonso pounced to send it into the net. Goal Liverpool! Tie game 3–3!

Milan fought back and nearly regained a lead at minute seventy. Dudek couldn't hold onto a low cross and Shevchenko sent a shot on goal, but the Reds defender Djimi Traore was standing on the goal line to clear the ball safely away. An incredibly close miss!

Kaká had the final chance to score before the end of the game, but he couldn't redirect Jaap Stam's header on goal. The game ended still tied. It would go to overtime.

Both teams had chances to score in extra time, and Milan came closest. Shevchenko sent a rocket on goal. Dudek made the save but the ball rebounded back to Milan's striker. Shevchenko fired again from point-blank six yards, but Dudek miraculously managed to deflect it over the bar. This game was going to a shootout.

Could Liverpool complete the unthinkable comeback? They now had an equal chance with penalty kicks. Milan's Serginho shot first and sent the ball sailing over the crossbar. Liverpool converted to take an edge. Andrea Pirlo was next for Milan, but Dudek dove to his right to make the save. Liverpool's Djibril Cisse scored on his attempt. Liverpool was up 2–0.

Milan converted its next kick, while Liverpool's next attempt was saved. Kaká stepped up next and scored to even the score at 2s. Liverpool's Šmicer regained the edge for Liverpool though, and the Rossoneri's Shevchenko was up. A goal would make Liverpool's final attempt a must-make to win. A miss would mean immediate victory for the Reds.

Shevchenko struck the ball down the center, counting on Dudek to dive to one side or the other. Dudek lunged to his right, but with his trailing left hand was able to block the rising ball. Save! Liverpool claimed the victory in a truly amazing comeback. The Reds were the champions of Europe.

The Rossoneri and their fans were heartbroken. "We had six minutes of madness in which we threw away the position we had reached until then," Coach Ancelotti said after the match. "We are unhappy, but I think we lost in an honorable way."

Kaká knew there was as much to learn in defeat as in victory—maybe more. It just wasn't nearly as much fun.

# Radical Reputation

Kaká had grown famous across Europe—mostly for his exceptional play on the field. But his reputation was intriguing to many people. He was the total opposite of the soccer star stereotype. Big magazines, newspapers, and TV shows across the continent wanted to tell his story. Readers and viewers wanted to know what was behind the carefree smile and game heroics. And Kaká wanted to tell them about the God he loved.

He continued to wear his Jesus bracelet everywhere he went, and it was widely known that he had the phrase "God is faithful" stitched into his cleats. The young Brazilian took every opportunity to reflect his gratitude and praise to Jesus. After goals he pointed and looked to the sky offering credit to God. When he spoke with reporters he was honest and outspoken about his love and devotion to Christ. He became famous for giving

Kaká, right, and World Food Program's representative John Powell show a jersey after Kaká was named an Ambassador Against Hunger by the U.N. World Food Program. Kaká was the agency's youngest ambassador in its campaign against global hunger.

generously to his church back home in Brazil, Renascer em Cristo, or Rebirth in Christ. With his huge salary, even a ten-percent tithe was a lot of money!

The playmaker also wanted to use his position of celebrity to serve others. "In Brazil we think we can help by using our image, the fact that we are very well known, to help others," Kaká said. He found the perfect way to make a difference when the United Nations World Food Program invited him to become their youngest ever Ambassador Against Hunger.

Kaká had first encountered extreme poverty in Brazil when he was twelve and visited a *favela* with his mother. Brazilian *favelas* are slums that are often ruled by drug lords. It opened his eyes to the blessings and comforts of his own life as well as the intense suffering and needs of others.

He realized how widespread the problems of hunger and poverty were when he traveled with the Seleção to play in some of the poorer areas of Brazil. "You see people come and watch us train or play a match and then you know some of them are going home with no food on the plate," he said.

Now he had an opportunity to raise awareness of the issues and try to bring help especially to children in poor countries. He worked with the U.N.'s Feed the World program and began visiting poor countries to try to bring hope and help find solutions. He also stayed connected to a ministry with his Brazilian church to help people fight drug abuse and avoid life on the streets.

The Rebirth in Christ church was the site of a happy occasion on December 23, 2005—Kaká and Caroline's wedding day. It was a beautiful and joyful event. Seven hundred guests joined the couple to celebrate, including many of Kaká's Milan and Brazil teammates. Longtime best friend Marcelo Saragosa stood beside Kaká as his best man, and Kaká even wrote a song to his bride for the occasion. Finally, after three years of dating and separation across the world, the couple were husband and wife.

Of course, the media in Brazil and Europe were interested in the festivities. The focus brought even more

Kaká with his bride, Caroline Celico, during their wedding in São Paulo, at the international headquarters of the Evangelical Church 'Renascer em Cristo' on December 23, 2005.

attention to Kaká and Caroline's faith, especially the fact that the couple had remained virgins until they were married. Sexual attitudes are generally loose in Brazil and Italy, and the fact was unbelievable that anyone— especially a superstar like Kaká—had actually followed God's commandments to keep sex only for marriage.

The couple spoke honestly about it, admitting that avoiding temptation hadn't been easy. "If today our life is so beautiful, I think it's also because we have been able to wait," Kaká told the Italian edition of *Vanity Fair* magazine.

Kaká and Caroline returned to Milan to make their new life together, continuing to serve God and represent him at every opportunity.

## Soccer vs. Football

Why is the sport called soccer in North America while most of the world calls it football? Many people think the name soccer was made up by Americans, but it actually originated in England. In 1863 there were a number of different "football" games being played with slightly different rules. The rules were standardized by England's Football Association. The game became known as Association Football to distinguish it from Rugby Football and others. Association Football was soon shortened into *soccer*, a type of abbreviation taken from "assoc." At the time, many of the upper class in England, including men who attended prestigious universities such as Oxford and Cambridge, called it soccer.

When the game became established in America, it was still often called football. In fact, the organization that governs soccer still had "football" in its name until 1974. The organization was first known as the U.S. Football Association (1913 – 1944), then U.S. Soccer Football Association (1945 – 1973), and finally U.S. Soccer Federation (1974 – current). Today the name "soccer" distinguishes the sport from American football, which has gained greater popularity in the United States.

## Toward the Goal

The U.S. isn't the only country to use the term "soccer." Canada, Ireland, and some in Australia, New Zealand, and South Africa use the term as well. But the majority of the world still prefers "football."

# Not-So-Magic in Germany

Kaká's on-field consolation after Milan's disappointments was Brazil's victorious Confederations Cup 2005. The prestigious tournament serves as a warm-up the year before each World Cup, and is limited to eight teams: the continental and regional champions of the world's soccer federations.

Brazil didn't look their best in the opening round, losing a close match to Mexico and tying Japan. But they did well enough to place second in the group and advance to the knockout rounds.

There the Canarinho edged mighty Germany 3–2 and thrashed their South American archrival Argentina 4–1 in the final. Kaká scored what turned out to be the winning goal in the sixteenth minute, and it has remained one of his favorites. "Every time you can score in a final, it's a completely different sensation from all the rest, and a fantastic feeling," he said later.

The championship was yet another reason why the defending World Cup champions were widely seen as favorites heading into Germany 2006. The Seleção boasted the globe's biggest collection of superstars on one team. At its center was the "magic quartet." Ronaldo was on the verge of becoming the all-time World Cup leading scorer. Ronaldinho had won the FIFA World Player of the Year award, given to the best player in the world, the previous two years. Adriano was a dangerous striker from Kaká's cross-town rival club Inter Milan. And Kaká had developed into a world superstar since being the young rookie at the Cup four years earlier.

Brazil expected a championship from its Seleção once again. The only question was: could the collection of superstars work smoothly as a team?

The answer seemed to be *maybe*, or at least well enough. In the first opening round game, Brazil edged out Croatia in a close match. The Croatians pressed the Brazilian defense and goalkeeper Dida was heroic with several big saves. Just before halftime Emerson surged onto Croatia's half of the field and passed to Cafu, who slipped the ball inside to Kaká. Kaká switched the ball to his left and fired an unstoppable curling shot from the edge of the box. It was Brazil's brightest moment and enough to give them a win.

After the match, Kaká told the press, "A narrow victory is good to calm down fans who think that there will always be goals and a spectacle, because this thing that

is said—that we are football's [Harlem] Globetrotters—
is just not true."

Brazil looked beatable, and they seemed to struggle to
gel their attack. But the Seleção built some momentum
with a 2–0 win over Australia, then finally seemed to find
its form with a 4–1 victory over Japan. It was Ronaldo's
breakout game of the Cup at last, and his two goals placed
him in a tie on the World Cup all-time leading scorer list.

Brazil won its group and moved to the knockout
round. Its foe in the quarterfinal match was Ghana, and
the Africans' defense was no match for the Brazilian attack. Ronaldo netted again to become the all-time leading World Cup scorer with fifteen lifetime goals.

The World Cup was down to eight teams, and Brazil
next faced France, an excellent team led by world stars
Zinedine Zidane and Thierry Henry. From the start the
French took control of the game, with playmaker Zidane
setting the pace. But they could not break through
Brazil's defense for any real scoring opportunities.

Kaká just missed a low cross from Ronaldo at the
near post in the fifteenth minute, but most of the first
half highlights came from Zidane's dazzling footwork.
Ronaldinho tried to match the fancy French footwork
early in the second half, but in the fifty-seventh minute,
France struck. Zidane floated a free kick from the left
side toward the far post. Henry was there to meet it with
the side of his right foot, and he volleyed the ball into the
goal. France took the lead 1–0.

With about thirty minutes left, Brazil changed its formation and shifted forward into its magic quartet. They

Associated Press/Luca Bruno

Kaká celebrates after scoring against Fenerbahce during the Champions League Group E match in Milan, Italy. Kaká's trademark gesture of raising his hands to the sky shows his thanks to God for the talent he has been given.

pressed the attack, trying to find the net, and later made even more offensive substitutions. Ronaldo attempted several shots, but France packed its defense back and thwarted every attempt. Brazil could find no answer for Les Bleus, and the defending champions were sent home to Brazil.

As the Cup continued without the Brazilians, France went all the way to the finals to play Italy for the title. France seemed to be the superior team, but the score remained tied 1–1 after regulation and overtime. In the end, the Italians prevailed on penalty kicks.

Brazil's Coach Parreira took the blame for the Samba Kings' defeat, and Ronaldo and Ronaldinho apologized for their overall lackluster performances.

After the opening game, Brazil's 1970 World Cup-winning captain Carlos Alberto told *The Guardian* newspaper, "Kaká was the only corner of the magic square that worked. The only way this tactical formation will be effective is if the players move around a lot. Ronaldinho tried to, but didn't manage. Ronaldo didn't do anything. Only Kaká managed to fit in."

The same consensus seemed to hold true for most of the Cup, but it was little consolation for him. "The World Cup was a huge frustration because I had prepared really hard for it," Kaká said later. "But in the World Cup there is no formula, no recipe for success."

Brazil's underachievement was blamed on the underwhelming performances of its biggest players. Of all its superstars in the magic quartet, it was only Kaká who had shone at all.

Both of his World Cups had defied original expectations. Both would serve as valuable learning experiences for different reasons.

## World Cup Records at a Glance
## (Prior to the start of the 2014 World Cup)

• Brazil is the only team to play at every one of the twenty World Cups (including 2014) and has won a record five championships.

• Ronaldo of Brazil is the overall leading goal scorer, with fifteen goals in three tournaments. He is followed by Germany's Gerd Müller with fourteen goals, France's Just Fontaine with thirteen goals, and Brazil's Pelé with twelve goals.

• Brazil has played ninety-seven matches, the most by any single nation. Germany has ninety-nine when the records of East and West Germany are combined.

• Brazil has scored 210 total goals, the most in the history of the World Cup.

• So far, only Brazil's Mário Zagallo and West Germany's Franz Beckenbauer have won the World Cup as both player and head coach.

• Highest match attendance in a World Cup final tournament is 199,854, when Uruguay played Brazil on July 16, 1950 in Maracanã Stadium, Rio de Janeiro, Brazil.

## Ronaldo

Ronaldo Luis Nazário de Lima, known as Ronaldo, is a favorite of Brazilian fans and considered to be their biggest soccer hero since Pelé. He rose to greatness in the 1990s and has played for a number of teams, including Internazionale, Real Madrid, AC Milan, and, of course, the Brazilian national team.

## Not-So-Magic in Germany

Ronaldo was named FIFA's World Player of the Year in 1996 and 1997. He was the youngest player to win the award as well as the first player to win the award two years in a row.

He has been part of Brazil's team in four World Cups:

• In 1994, at the age of seventeen, he was on the championship team but didn't play.

• In 1998 he gave a star performance but was criticized for Brazil's loss in the final.

• In 2002 he led Brazil to a World Cup championship and won the Golden Boot as the tournament's top scorer with eight goals.

• In 2006, despite accusations of being overweight and slow, he scored three goals for a lifetime total of fifteen in World Cup play — a new record.

Ronaldo returned to Brazil to play with Corinthians until his retirement in 2011. He is remembered for playing with Brazilian flair and remains an ambassador for Brazilian soccer.

# Golden Year

2007 was Kaká's year. When Milan's striker Andriy Shevchenko departed for the English Premier League's Chelsea in the off-season, more responsibility fell to the twenty-four-year-old Kaká.

The team struggled a bit trying to find the right balance in its attack. Then Coach Ancelotti tried a new formation, with Kaká and Clarence Seedorf pushed forward as the main attackers.

At first, Kaká felt "a bit mesmerized," as he later described. His role had always been to create goal-scoring situations for the forwards. Now he was on the receiving end of most passes, expected to finish with the ball in the net.

"I have learned to have the mentality of a striker, because before I had a midfielder's mentality, and I still do, which is that of making the last pass," Kaká told *World*

*Soccer* later. "But forwards don't work that way. So now I have to finish the move myself."

Like most things involving a soccer ball, Kaká picked up his new role quite well, though he claimed after the season that he still wasn't fully comfortable as a striker. That didn't keep him from scoring ten goals in Serie A, enough to make him the league leader.

But his most important strikes came during Champions League play. Milan advanced through UEFA group play as one of sixteen teams with a chance to claim the title. There, the Rossoneri first faced the Celtics from the Scottish Premier League. Champions League knock-out rounds consist of teams playing each other twice for points, with each getting one home game. In the first match in Glasgow, Scotland, the two clubs battled to a scoreless tie. Back at the San Siro, things looked similar as the clock wound down. Neither team had been able to find the net.

Kaká came ever-so-close in the eighty-seventh minute. He chipped the ball from twenty yards and sent it sailing over the head of Celtic's goalkeeper Artur Boruc. Boruc was beat. It looked like the ball was going in — but it struck the crossbar and bounced clear.

The game went to overtime. Three minutes into the extra period Milan took the ball and launched a fast counterattack. Marek Jankulovski served the ball to Kaká at midfield. Kaká dribbled at a sprint past one defender, then outran two more toward the left post. As Boruc moved out to challenge and a Celtic defender tried to slide tackle, Kaká drove the ball between Boruc's legs for the goal that would prove to be the winner.

The Rossoneri moved through the Champions League, beating Celtic and Bayern Munich to set up a duel with mighty Manchester United. Manchester United is one of the most dominant teams in the English Premiere League and regularly one of the world's best. It is arguably the most famous team in the world, with an estimated 75 million fans who claim the Red Devils as their team.

What's intimidating is Old Trafford, United's home stadium, where 74,000 red-clad fans sing and chant for their team beneath banners that read *Manchester United The Religion*. That's where Milan would have to play first.

Besides being a clash between two of the world's top clubs, this pair of games was seen as a duel between two of the world's brightest young stars: Kaká and Cristiano Ronaldo. Ronaldo was United's Portuguese striker, who had an exceptional knack for finding the net. At the time he was on the verge of an astonishing forty-two goals. He played with a sensational flair, relying on quick dribbling and fancy footwork, and he had a reputation for being fiery and demanding. In many ways, he was the exact opposite of the smooth, straightforward Kaká.

United was heavily favored. The Red Devils were on the way to claiming the Premier League title back home in England. They had already won the prestigious FA Cup. Manchester also had beaten its last Champions League opponent, Roma, 7–1.

Against Milan, Ronaldo struck quickly for the English side, deflecting a corner kick into the back of the net only five minutes into the game. But then the game turned into Kaká's show. He found the net for Milan in the twenty-second minute to tie the score. With a beautiful dribble, he sped into the box past two United defenders and sent the ball inside the far post from an amazing angle.

United didn't let up its attack, though, and Milan's Dida was forced to make several diving saves. Kaká struck again in the thirty-seventh minute to give Milan a 2–1 lead at halftime. As he raced for the ball, so did two United defenders. Kaká managed to head the ball forward and sidestep around as they crashed into each other. With only the goalie left, Kaká shot a roller past his dive and inside the post.

Manchester United found the net next when Wayne Rooney shot past Dida from eighteen yards out. The game remained tied past the regulation ninety minutes before United launched a fast counterattack in the extra three minutes the ref added to make up for injury delays. Ryan Giggs sprinted down the right wing with the ball, passed it inside to Rooney near the corner of the box. Rooney smashed it inside the near post and into the net. It was a dramatic 3–2 win for Manchester United.

A week later the clubs squared off again, this time in San Siro. Kaká was determined to see a different result. Milan's Champions League's hopes depended on it.

Playing in the pouring rain, Kaká picked right back up with his scoring, giving Milan the lead just eleven minutes into the game. Clarence Seedorf headed a ball to the center, where the rushing Kaká charged and fired a low volley past the goalie, Edwin van der Sar. A few minutes later it was Seedorf's turn, using his chest to control a cross from the right side, then firing the ball past van der Sar. Later Alberto Gilardino made it 3–0 Milan when he sprinted into the penalty box alone and easily looped the ball into the goal in a one-on-one against van der Sar.

The game was all Milan—and all Kaká. His presence and playmaking was dominant throughout both games, and Manchester United had been unable to contain him. It was later called the greatest moment of his career, even more so than the coming Champions League final.

By splitting the games with a victory a piece, the determining factor between the two teams was the number of goals scored, and Milan had the edge 5–3. The Rossoneri were headed to the Champions League final.

For some time now, Kaká had been talked about as one of the best players in the world. Now the official awards began pouring in. Some of the most prestigious were the Ballon d'Or, or Golden Ball, given to the best player in the world, and the FIFPro World Player of the Year, voted on by more than fifty thousand soccer professionals around the world.

On December 17, 2007, Kaká walked onto the stage at the Zurich Opera House in Switzerland, where the Brazilian legend Pelé handed him the award for FIFA World Player of the Year, the most prestigious honor in soccer.

Kaká, left, receives the trophy from soccer legend Pelé after being named FIFA World Player of the Year during the 17th FIFA World Player Gala in Zurich, Switzerland, December 17, 2007.

The recognition signaled that Kaká was the prime example of the new global soccer star at his peak. Many Latin Americans, especially Brazilians, had reached the top levels of European soccer. But from the start Kaká was a rare combination of the best of both worlds: the elegant creativity of South America mixed with the tactical strategy of Europe. Kaká's game is both beautiful and smart. His incredible ball-controlling skills are used more often to make an amazing assist for a teammate's goal, but his own dangerous shooting and scoring keeps opposing goalkeepers on edge.

The honors brought the star player great satisfaction, but he received them all with his normal humility and gratitude. In all his acceptance speeches and interviews, he genuinely thanked God, his family, his coaches, and his teammates. Kaká recognized that he wouldn't be accepting all of the trophies without the help of great teammates.

With the sign of a great champion, Kaká knew that his awards didn't mean he was a perfect player. If anything, they fueled his desire to keep working hard. "My aim is to keep on listening and learning from others and to keep improving as a player and as a person," Kaká said after receiving the FIFPro trophy. "It is a privilege to be a professional footballer, and it is our duty to work hard to be the best we can be for our teammates, supporters, club, and country, and to earn the respect of fellow men."

When asked later by *World Soccer* magazine if his Champions League victory had been the most important game of his life, Kaká answered, "No. The most important match in my life will always be the next one. You mustn't dwell too much on what has been achieved — or else you run the risk of losing motivation."

Kaká was also motivated to keep his priorities in order: faith, family, then football. On the verge of winning his Champions League title with Milan, he said, "The best goal of my life would be to become a father

Marucia Kintschev/AFP/Getty Images

Kaká with his wife, Caroline, and son, Luca, in São Paulo, Brazil, on June 10, 2008.

and hold my first child in my arms." Some medical problems made that difficult for Caroline. But a little over a year later, she gave birth to their son, Luca, on June 10, 2008.

"It is such a great joy for me to be able to say today that I am the father of such a wonderful son, the husband of such a wonderful wife, and that I am part of a blessed family," Kaká said.

The footballing father's attitude on and off the field all but ensured that the world had plenty yet to expect from Kaká, its most superior player.

## FIFA Ballon d'Or — World Player of the Year

Since 1956 journalists have been voting to award the Golden Ball to the best player in the world. The Ballon d'Or started as an honor only for European players in a European club, but has come to be awarded to any player of any nationality. In 2010, the award was merged into a single honor with the FIFA World Player of the Year. Journalists, national coaches, and captains all vote.

# Not About the Money

The breaking news rocked the soccer world. Manchester City was offering AC Milan more than 100 million British pounds, or $146 million, to let Kaká come play for their team in the English Premier League. And if the deal went through, Kaká would earn a half million dollars each *week*.

It was an astronomical sum even in the high-dollar world of soccer—or any pro sport, for that matter. The offer would more than double the previous record for the highest transfer fee: $65 million for Zinedine Zidane at Real Madrid in 2001. However, the Manchester City team had been purchased earlier in the year by Sheikh Mansour bin Zayed al-Nahyan. He came from the royal family of Abu Dhabi, an oil-rich nation in the Middle East. He was willing to spare no expense to turn his team into a winner.

Kaká's initial response was that he loved playing at Milan and hoped to stay and eventually become captain of the team—but that the decision lay first with his club. In contract negotiations, a player's team owned the first right to decide whether to consider another team's offer. If Milan agreed, then Manchester City could talk directly with Kaká about making the move.

Milan loved its star player but was facing economic difficulties in the midst of the global economic recession. If they sold Kaká's contract, it would help them to balance their own budget and free up money for them to bring in other rising stars for less money. Manchester City's offer was too much for them to pass up, so Milan's executives agreed to the deal if Kaká said yes.

Milan's fans, on the other hand, were outraged. They protested in the streets outside Milan's headquarters and outside Kaká's house, waving banners and chanting for their star to stay with the Rossoneri. They loved their Brazilian star, and he loved them. One night he appeared at his window, waving down to the fans and holding a Milan jersey to his heart. Indeed, Kaká and Caroline had put down roots in their Italian city, and Kaká had even received Italian citizenship.

As negotiations continued with Kaká and his father, who was his professional agent, the soccer world speculated about what would happen. His former Brazilian national coach, Luiz Felipe Scolari, offered wise insight when he told the Associated Press, "I know Kaká very well. Money is not his problem."

Kaká prayed about the decision and discussed it with

his loved ones. In the end, Scolari was correct. Kaká announced he would turn down the exorbitant amount of money to stay in Milan. "All the messages that I received said to choose with the heart, and I think in the end that has been the decision," Kaká said. "It is absolutely not about money."

Milan rejoiced, and Kaká seemed relieved to return his attention to simply playing the game he loved. But the door had been opened to negotiate with Milan's star, and other clubs were quick to knock. Rumors swirled about another high bid from Chelsea, one of the Big Four teams from the English Premier League, but the attempted deal went nowhere.

Then came word that Real Madrid was in the mix, and in June 2009 it was official. Kaká was headed to play for the storied club in the Primera Division of the Liga de Futbol Profesional, better known as Spain's La Liga, another one of the strongest professional soccer leagues in the world. Although not as much as Manchester City's bid, 65 million Euros, or about $93 million, set a new record for the highest transfer fee ever.

Yet Kaká insisted that his decision had more to do with the possibilities of more championships on the field than his paycheck. "I knew I'd only leave Milan to play for Real," he told the BBC. "It's an important project for me to continue growing in my career. I'm not going to Real Madrid for money, as I had other offers. That's why I chose Madrid. They have historic players there already, such as Raul and Iker Casillas. It will be an important challenge for me. We're going to win many titles again."

Winning championships was something Real Madrid was known for. The club has a record thirty-two La Liga championships and nine European Cup/UEFA Champions League titles, also a record. The team was named the best club of the twentieth century after a detailed study of statistics by the International Federation of Football Statistics (IFFHS).

The Whites, as they are also called, had their last great era in 2000, when club leadership paid big dollars to bring in superstars, including Ronaldo, David Beckham, Zinedine Zidane, Luis Figo, Roberto Carlos, and Raul. It was the world's biggest collection of top talent in one place, and the group was known as the Galacticos. The team's emphasis was on overpowering other teams with its superpowered offense. The Galacticos era brought La Liga titles in 2001 and 2003, and a European Super Cup in 2002.

The 2008–2009 season saw rival Barcelona dominate La Liga, and Real Madrid brought back Florentino Perez, the club president who had assembled the Galacticos. He took the same strategy: the world's biggest dollars for the world's biggest players.

Kaká was the first blockbuster deal, but a few days later, 2008's World Player of the Year Cristiano Ronaldo was signed to Madrid. His deal broke the record set on Kaká, and 80 million pounds, or $129 million, made Cristiano Ronaldo the most expensive soccer player ever. The world's two best players were now teammates.

U.S. and English Premier League goalkeeper Tim Howard had faced both players—and tried to stop them from scoring. "[Kaká] is one of the two best players in the world," he said during the Confederations Cup. "He's amazing because most of what he does is without flair. I think Cristiano Ronaldo is the other best player in the world, but he does it with flair. With Kaká, everything seems to be so simple for him, which is frustrating."

Real Madrid didn't stop with those two. Soon the club added even more star power. Karim Benzema came from Olympique Lyonnais in France, and Xabi Alonso arrived from Liverpool to serve as the defensive anchor of the midfield. The total reached nine new players brought in, as well as coach Manuel Pelligrini.

Talk began right away of a new Galacticos II era led by Kaká and Cristiano Ronaldo. But neither liked the comparison. They preferred to establish their own new era, hopefully of success.

Kaká especially knew the importance of being more than a collection of star players. From the start he urged his teammates to put aside big egos and work hard.

"My experience in football tells me that talent is not enough. The Brazilian national team in 2006 had a lot of talent, but we were knocked out of the World Cup quarter-finals because we lacked many things which prevented us from succeeding," Kaká told *The Independent*. "Real Madrid have Cristiano and Benzema, and that's good because we are quality players, but we need to build a team and work very hard. Real Madrid won't become invincible just by signing us."

On June 30, Kaká walked through the tunnel into Real Madrid's historic stadium, the Bernabéu, in his official Real Madrid uniform. There was no game to be played—yet. But there were 50,000 fans in the stands cheering as their new player was introduced. It was a hero's welcome in Kaká's new playing home.

## Santiago Bernabéu Stadium

Built in 1944, the stadium is named after the club's chairman at the time who had a vision for giving the fans of Real Madrid an amazing stadium to match their team. It currently holds 80,000 seated spectators, down from the 125,000 seated and standing spectators in the 1950s. It has hosted many exciting tournaments, including European Cup finals, European Nations' Cup, and the 1982 World Cup. While soccer is the main attraction here, the stadium occasionally hosts concerts as well.

## Real Madrid

Full team name: Real Madrid Club de Fútbol
Nicknames: Many, including *Los Merengues* (which is a delicious cake of the rich), *Los Vikingos* (The Vikings), and *Los Blancos* (The Whites, because of their uniforms).
Home stadium: Santiago Bernabéu, Madrid, Spain
League: La Liga
Founded: 1902
Main opponents: FC Barcelona and Atlético de Madrid
Honors:

• Has won the most European Cup/UEFA Champions League titles: nine.

• Ranked the richest club in the world based on revenue by *Forbes* in 2013.

• Called "the most successful football club of the twentieth century" by FIFA.

• Named the best club of the 20th century after an in-depth study by the International Federation of Football History and Statistics (IFFHS).

## Cristiano Ronaldo

Cristiano Ronaldo dos Santos Aveiro is a forward for Real Madrid and the captain of Portugal's national team. He is widely considered one of the best players in the world. Prior to coming to Spain, "CR7" played for Manchester United in England from the age of eighteen. He was named the FIFA World Player of the Year in 2008 and has finished runner-up for the top award in 2009, 2011, and 2012. Cristiano Ronaldo is always a dangerous scoring threat due to his astonishing speed, dazzling ball control, and powerful shooting ability. He holds several Real Madrid scoring records, including most goals in a season: sixty, which he scored in 2011–2012. He was nicknamed Ronaldo after Ronald Reagan, his father's favorite actor.

## The Spanish Liga

The top professional league in Spain is called The Primera División (First Division) of the Liga de Fútbol Profesional (Professional Football League). It is more commonly called La Liga. As in many other professional leagues, they adopt the relegation system where the three lowest ranked teams are

relegated to a lower division, while the three highest-ranked teams from the lower division are promoted to La Liga.

The Big Two, Real Madrid and Barcelona, have traditionally dominated the competition with Real edging Barca in overall league titles 32–22. Atlético Madrid or Athletic Bilbao often rounds out the top three.

# Champions Heading for the World Cup

This was not a place Brazil was used to being: losing at halftime—to the United States, no less. The Americans had played two brilliant games to reach this final of the 2009 Confederations Cup, but they were not one of the world's traditional soccer powers.

The Confederations Cup is an elite tournament held every four years in the year before the World Cup. The champions of each world soccer region, plus the current World Cup champion and the host country, make up the eight teams who play.

Brazil was the reigning champion of the South American Football Confederation, better known as CONMEBOL. It was also the defending Confederations Cup champion. The United States had won the Confederation of North, Central American, and Caribbean Association Football (CONCACAF).

Brazil's first game had been against a tenacious Egypt. The Seleção jumped to a 3–1 lead by halftime, but the Pharoahs fought back to tie. Egypt brought it even again ten minutes into the second half. The match seemed destined for a tie. But when an Egyptian player touched the ball with his hands, Brazil was awarded a penalty kick. Kaká got the ball into the goal, giving Brazil a narrow victory.

The Canarinho rolled through its next two opening round games, dismantling the United States 3–0 and Italy 3–0. It seemed the Brazilians were back to their unbeatable selves.

The host nation, South Africa, played tougher than expected in the semifinal match, and it took a late curling free kick in the final two minutes to find the net and seal another victory for the Brazilians.

On the other side of the bracket, the United States faced off against Spain, the number one team in the world. Everyone expected a Brazil–Spain showdown in the final.

The Americans had struggled early in the tournament, losing 1–3 to Italy and 0–3 to Brazil. Going into their last first-round game against Egypt, the Yanks had an extremely slim chance to claim second place in its group and enable them to advance. If the U.S. could beat Egypt by three *and* if Italy lost to Brazil by three, then the U.S. could advance on a mathematical tie-breaker. It was a long shot—but it was a shot.

The Americans knew anything can happen in international soccer—and it did. The United States won 3–0.

Brazil beat Italy 3–0. Amazingly, the U.S. moved on. The final was set for a Brazil versus United States rematch. Could the Americans find yet another miracle?

Riding their never-say-die euphoria from the Spain victory, the Americans came out hard and strong and netted first only ten minutes into the game. Brazil seemed stunned and flat, and the Americans dominated the first half, taking a 2–0 lead into the locker room at halftime. The Brazilians remained optimistic. "We can do it," they told each other. "We can turn the match around. Let's go."

The second half was a completely different story. It only took one minute in the second half for Luis Fabiano to score for Brazil. Kaká took control and began to orchestrate a Brazilian attack that sent the Americans reeling. The shots began to flow for the Seleção. Tim Howard, the American goalie, made spectacular saves, but the momentum was flowing green and gold.

In the sixtieth minute, Kaká headed a ball off the underside of the crossbar before Howard grabbed it. The Brazilians called for a goal. The referee said to play on. TV replays showed that the ball had indeed crossed the goal line, but there are no instant replays in soccer. The U.S. held its narrow lead, even when Luis Fabiano's pointblank blast was saved by Howard.

Fifteen minutes from the end of regulation play, Kaká carried the ball down the left wing, eluded defender Jonathan Spector, and crossed to Elano. The shot struck the crossbar, bounced back in front of the goal, and was headed in by Luis Fabiano. Tie game.

Both teams pushed hard to find a winning goal. Five minutes before the end of regulation, Brazil was awarded a corner kick. Elano struck a beautiful cross that curved away from the goal to the back corner of the penalty box. Lucio leaped over Clint Dempsey and headed a rocket between the post and a lunging Howard. Brazil had battled back to win 3–2.

As the Brazilians danced and celebrated their victory, some of the Americans wept openly. Kaká wore his trademark "I belong to Jesus" T-shirt alongside Lucio in his own "I love Jesus." The comeback victory showed the resilience and heart of the skilled Brazilian squad.

Kaká was given the Golden Ball award in the ceremony following the game. Teammate Luis Fabiano claimed the Golden Shoe for overall leading scorer. And the entire Brazilian team received the Fair Play Award for their graceful play and enthusiastic sportsmanship.

As usual, Kaká deflected praise to his teammates. "The most important thing, as I've always said, is to win as a unit. All of that happened and Brazil was the champion," he said following the final match. "If it hadn't been for the team I wouldn't have been the best player or the man of the match."

The victory helped to secure Brazil as a favorite heading into the 2010 World Cup in South Africa. It also gave Brazilian fans confidence in their Seleção.

After its disappointing 2006 World Cup, Dunga took over as coach and shook up the squad. He benched all the superstars, including Ronaldo, Ronaldinho, and even Kaká, making it clear that everyone must earn their spot based on hard work and solid performance. Dunga had been the captain of the 1994 World Cup champions team, and, as a player, was known as a tough defender. As a coach he emphasized disciplined, tactical soccer, and many Brazilians criticized and complained, claiming that their Seleção was no longer playing the improvised but beautiful game Brazil had always been known for.

Of course, Kaká emerged as just the type of player to lead the re-made Brazilians with his mix of fundamental skills, efficient passing, and killer scoring ability. Just before their Confederations Cup showdown, the American star Landon Donovan described Kaká like this, "When they are comfortable in possession, he does a good job of just moving the ball and keeping things going. And then when he sees an opportunity with some space to go, he takes off and he's gone. He makes the right pass, he's good in front of the goal. Physically, he's so gifted. You forget that he's so big, he's strong, and how fast he is. In a lot of ways, he's the ideal soccer player."

Still the team struggled with some of its early international results but built solid momentum in 2009 by winning the Confederations Cup and securing qualification for the World Cup. And the more they won, the more the demanding nation of Brazil began to believe in the new vision of its team. But they expected nothing less than a championship in South Africa.

Kaká said it was his number one goal for 2010. But he and his teammates knew the road would be long to reach that destination. And first came a season with the new Galacticos in Spain.

## Dunga

Carlos Caetano Bledorn Verri, better known as Dunga, is a former Brazilian defensive midfielder known for a tough, no-nonsense playing style — different than the artistic, beautiful game Brazilians love. He anchored the team defense for its 1994 World Cup victory.

As the coach of Brazil's national team from 2006 to 2010, he emphasized hard teamwork over individual stardom. Many Brazilians criticized him for it, claiming he tried to turn the Seleção into a European-style team.

## South Africa: Host of the World Cup 2010

• The Republic of South Africa is located on the southern tip of the continent.

• The government is a democracy, with the president as the head of state.

• The country is rich with natural beauty: lakes, mountains, hills, coast, and plains.

• It is known as the Rainbow Nation. This refers to the richness of the people of South Africa — diverse cultures, histories, and languages. While English is most commonly used in official business, there are eleven officially recognized languages.

• Football is sometimes called soccer and colloquially referred to as *diski*.

• South Africa's history was marked by violent racist political and economic policy that discriminated against non-whites. This system of government was called Apartheid.

## Champions Heading for the World Cup

• South Africa was banned from international soccer competition for nearly three decades because of Apartheid.

• Since 1992 when it was allowed to play again, South Africa has shown its strength and talent in international soccer.

# Reality at Real

Having the best players doesn't always mean having the best team. Brazil's star-studded national team discovered that at the 2006 World Cup. Real Madrid would have to realize the same, but it would take time and work to get used to playing as a team.

Part of good teamwork is filling different roles. Cristiano Ronaldo is a striker who attacks the goal with lethal speed and power. Gonzalo Higuaín and Karim Benzema are also speedy, lethal scorers. Having those forwards up front allowed Kaká to start in the center as attacking midfielder and playmaker, a natural and comfortable position for him.

The team started strong, winning its first seven games of the season. Those victories included two solid victories in the UEFA Champions League: a 5–2 win over Zurich from Switzerland and a 3–0 defeat over the French squad Marseilles.

But October was rough on Los Blancos. The team experienced its first loss in La Liga and its first Champions League loss to Kaká's former club, AC Milan. But the loss to tiny Alcorcón in the first round of the *Copa del Rey*, or King's Cup, hurt the most.

The Copa del Rey is the oldest tournament in Spain. The prestigious competition includes teams from all levels of Spain's professional leagues. Alcorcón was basically a minor league team. It played in the third tier, the Spanish Second Division B—the same division as Real Madrid's youth team. That didn't stop the overwhelming underdog from beating mighty Real. The tiny David of a team didn't just squeak out a victory. It took down Madrid Goliath-style with a 4–0 thumping. Alcorcón called it their greatest victory ever. Media and fans called it Real Madrid's worst humiliation in the club's long history.

Coach Manuel Pelligrini had chosen to rest Kaká along with fellow starting midfielder Xabi Alonso and goalkeeper Iker Casillas. Cristiano Ronaldo was also out for several games due to an ankle injury. The team was struggling without him, but it still had plenty of skill and star power on the field—or should have.

Newspapers and websites called for Coach Pelligrini to be fired. Madridistas had high expectations. They demanded trophies and championships, not embarrassment. Their club had spent millions, and they would not be patient to see it pay off.

Similar to the World Cup and Champions League, each round of the Copa del Rey includes two games. Kaká returned to the lineup for the second match, but Madrid could only muster a 1–0 win over Alcorcón. It was not nearly enough to make up for the first loss. Real Madrid was eliminated from the Copa del Rey.

"We hope our fans can forgive us," Pelligrini said.

Madrid's director general Jorge Valdano backed his coach, but said, "We have to take it as a lesson in humility that must serve as a starting point for a fresh beginning."

There was still plenty of time left in the season. Real was still alive in the Champions League and took the lead in La Liga with a victory in its next game. Up next was Spanish archrival FC Barcelona. As is usually the case, this bitter rivalry would be the key to the season.

These two clubs are the giants of Spain. Their rivalry is one of the biggest in the world, and they have played each other for well over a hundred years. They come from Spain's largest cities. Of the eighty-two titles in the history of La Liga, these two teams have won fifty-four combined, as of the 2012-2013 season. Real Madrid leads with thirty-two championships. Barcelona has twenty-two.

Each game the Big Two play is called *El Clásico*, or The Classic. Heading into the first matchup of 2009, Madrid held a one-point lead in the league. Cristiano Ronaldo returned to the lineup after his injury. A victory would mean three valuable points over Barca, the reigning league champion, but Los Blancos would have to claim it on the road at Barcelona's enormous stadium, Camp Nou.

Real Madrid played almost perfectly, attacking the Barca goal again and again. Almost twenty minutes into the game, Kaká made a spectacular move and fed the ball to Cristiano Ronaldo. It took a stunning save from the feet of Barca goalkeeper Victor Valdez to keep the ball out of the net. But that was the story of night. Madrid couldn't get a goal. Barcelona was able to score one. Los Blancos looked strong, but Barcelona overtook first place.

Worse, Kaká aggravated a groin injury in the game. He had been playing through the pain of the muscle problem for a while. Now it was bad enough to knock him out of competition. "In my day it nearly always required an operation, but now there are other types of treatments which are much better," Madrid's sports director Miguel Pardeza said. "I am sure he will be back with us again very soon."

But Kaká would miss a month of games. And the injury would haunt him for a long time to come.

Madrid reclaimed the league lead in March. But the team was eliminated from the Champions League that same month by France's Lyon. Kaká reinjured his groin muscle in that European showdown and was knocked out of competition for another six weeks.

Even without him, Los Merengues held the league lead through March—until the second Clásico of the season. Again the night belonged to Barcelona. Goals by Lionel Messi and Pedro Rodgríquez secured a 2–0 win for the visitors in the Bernabéu. The league lead also went back to Barca by three points.

Remember that number. Mathematically it was still possible for Real Madrid to win the championship with seven games remaining.

Kaká made a heroic return with five games left. He came on as a late sub against Real Zaragoza. With only seven minutes to play, Kaká cut across the middle of the box and received a pass from Cristiano Ronaldo. One dribble. Two dribbles. And with a defender on his back, Kaká shot across the goalmouth and scored the winner in the 2–1 victory.

Real Madrid did its part, winning the rest of its games. But so did Barcelona. Going into the last game of the season, Barcelona held a one-point lead. If Barca lost or tied and Madrid won, the title would belong to Real Madrid. It was the only way the Whites could be champions. But Barcelona secured a victory, and Madrid could only muster a 1–1 tie with Malaga. Barcelona was La Liga champion for the second year in a row.

The season was historic for Real Madrid. Its ninety-six total La Liga points was a club record, but all that mattered was that it was three points behind the champions. The club had entered the season with the highest hopes and expectations. This team had been assembled to win trophies. Anything less was failure. And failure would bring certain changes to the club.

"I'm not happy with my performance, but my problem is physical," Kaká said, referencing his injuries. "I have suffered a lot since I arrived."

But for now, Kaká and his superstar teammates would have to put their disappointment behind them. The World Cup was coming within months. Soccer's greatest prize was still on the line. Reclaiming that championship for Brazil would make up for Spanish disappointments.

## El Clásico

Sports rivalries don't come any bigger than Real Madrid versus Barcelona. The clubs represent the two largest cities in Spain. Their fans generally represent different political viewpoints: Madrid, the capital, represents nationalism. Barcelona is in the Catalan region, which often supports its own independence. The Big Two are the richest, mightiest teams in La Liga, and neither has ever been relegated out of the first division.

The Whites have played the Blaugrana, or Scarlet and Blue, 257 total times, as of the end of the 2012-2013 season. Counting only official games, Real Madrid leads the all-time series 90 to 86. Count all matches and Barcelona has the edge, 105–94. Each head-to-head match is almost guaranteed to be a classic.

## FC Barcelona

Full team name: Football Club Barcelona
Nicknames: Barca or Blaugrana (the Scarlet and Blue because of their uniforms)
Home stadium: Camp Nou, Barcelona, Spain

# Toward the Goal

League: La Liga
Founded: 1899
Motto: More than a club
Main opponents: Real Madrid
Honors:

• Has won La Liga twenty-two times and the European Cup/ UEFA Champions League four times.

• In 2009, became the first club to win the Treble in one season: La Liga, Copa del Rey, and the Champions League.

• That same year became the first team ever to win the Sextuple, winning the Treble plus the Spanish Super Cup, UEFA Super Cup, and FIFA Club World Cup.

# Back to the World Cup

The Brazilian nation's expectations were as high as ever heading into the FIFA World Cup 2010 in South Africa: Bring home the golden trophy as champions of the world for the sixth time—and look good doing it.

But the soccer-crazed country was nervous about this rendition of the Seleção. Yes, the Confederations Cup championship had satisfied fans. But the more tactical, conservative style under Coach Dunga still had critics. The creative flair of *jogo bonita* was missing, critics claimed. Could their beloved Canarinho win without its creative heart?

"We have to learn to live with the favorites' tag," Kaká had said after a historic 3–1 win in Argentina secured qualification. "We mustn't let it turn into something negative, as it has done in previous years."

It didn't help that Brazil had been drawn into the

Group of the Death for the opening round. To advance, Brazil would have to best powerful Portugal, led by Kaká's Real Madrid teammate Cristiano Ronaldo. They would also have to overcome Ivory Coast and its megastar striker Didier Drogba. The Ivorians were especially inspired by the hope of winning the first World Cup ever to be held on African soil. The fourth team in Group G was not a favorite, but the Democratic People's Republic of Korea, better known as North Korea, was a tenacious team that could not be taken lightly.

Kaká was the lynchpin and leader of Brazil. He was the veteran playmaker in midfield, and Brazil had never lost a game when he had scored. But Kaká was surrounded by the attacking skills of forwards Robinho and Luis Fabiano and the experienced defending anchors of Maicon and Lucio. Together they echoed their coach and called on their country to support the team.

"To make changes would only drive us away from our path," defender Dani Alves said. "We are on the right track, and we have to finish in the same manner."

In other words, winning was the most important goal even if it didn't always look pretty.

Brazil's opening game against North Korea didn't start as the prettiest. The Korean underdogs lived up to their reputation for tough defense. Kaká made a dangerous run into Korea's penalty box in the early minutes but was swarmed before he could shoot. The Brazilians controlled the ball but had to settle for long shots. Some looked dangerous but sailed high or wide. Halftime came with a scoreless tie.

Ten minutes into the second half, Maicon chased down a long pass that seemed to be overhit. The ball was only a foot or two from rolling out of bounds over the touchline when Maicon slammed a shot across the goal. The angle was impossible. Yet the ball screamed between the goalkeeper and the near post and curved into the goal. Elano added to Brazil's lead seventeen minutes later. A late goal by North Korea wasn't enough. Brazil had its first victory of the 2010 World Cup.

The next opponent was Ivory Coast. Many experts predicted the Elephants, led by megastar Didier Drogba, would be Africa's best chance of a home-continent champion. But if Brazil was nervous, they didn't show it. Rhythm flowed for the Samba Boys. Robinho, Luis Fabiano, and Kaká worked beautifully together in the 3–1 victory.

Unfortunately, in the final minutes Abdelkader Keïta charged at Kaká away from the ball. Kaká raised his forearm to shield himself and blocked Keita across the chest. But Keita fell to the ground clutching his face and rolling around. Out came the referee's yellow card. Instead of giving it to Keita for diving, the referee carded Kaká. It was his second yellow of the game, so it equaled a red. Kaká was sent off the field. Replays clearly showed no contact with Keita's face.

"It was a totally unjustified dismissal of Kaká," Dunga said after the game. "He was fouled, and yet he was punished."

"I prefer to let the pictures speak for themselves," Kaká said.

The incident hurt. It meant that Kaká would have to miss the next game against Portugal. He was disappointed but searched for the positive as Dunga searched for his replacement.

"I think I can be a good example for the others in terms of showing that I'm willing to work hard," Kaká said. "I can help them by giving them advice and also through my attitude. The fact that I'm not playing will be a great motivation for whoever takes my place in the team, and I hope that they play well and enjoy good fortune because the game against Portugal will be tough."

Portugal was expected to be the toughest opponent yet. They had just dismantled North Korea 7–0. Brazil was relieved that they would advance to the knockout rounds no matter what happened against Portugal.

Besides sharing the Portuguese language, the two teams shared a similar playing style. Both coaches also made changes to their lineups and formations, with Portugal adding a fifth midfielder. Brazil possessed the ball more often, but Portugal created the most dangerous scoring possibilities, thanks to Cristiano Ronaldo. The game stayed mostly clogged in the midfield, and it ended in a 0–0 tie. Both teams were satisfied.

Brazil had won the Group of Death. Now came the do-or-die Round of Sixteen. Up first was South American rival Chile. The two were well acquainted with each other, but Brazil took charge of their World Cup matchup. The Seleção rolled to a 3–0 victory. The dominant performance showed why they were a World Cup favorite.

"Some people doubted that we would perform, but as we go along that confidence is growing and growing," Dunga said. "We hope to make it to the final."

Meanwhile, the Netherlands did its part to earn a date with Brazil by putting away Slovakia 2–1. The Dutch team was loaded with talent, including Arjen Robben, Wesley Sneijder, Dirk Kuyt and Robin van Persie. Yet as the game got going, it looked like Brazil's roll would continue past their Dutch opponents. Robinho struck the back of the net within the first few minutes but was ruled offside—no goal. But in the tenth minute, he perfectly timed a through-ball down the middle from Felipe Melo to convert a goal. Brazil held the 1–0 lead into halftime, but it was a narrow margin against the likes of the *Oranje,* the Orange.

Both teams threatened with exceptional skill, but shots flew wide or into goalkeepers' gloves. Then eight minutes after halftime, Sneijder sent a long cross from the right side. It looked harmless, but Brazil's goalkeeper, Julio Cesar, hesitated for a second. He charged out to punch the ball away. At the same time, Felipe Melo leaped for the ball. The ball glanced off his head. Cesar missed. Into the back of the net it went. A mistake by Brazil—a goal for the Netherlands.

Until that moment, Brazil had been looking its best of the World Cup. They were playing confident and elegant soccer. Another victory seemed to be theirs for the taking, despite the Dutch team's physical challenges and perseverance. But that surprise goal turned the tide for the Oranje.

Brazil didn't give up. Kaká sent a volley screaming past the post soon after. But the Netherlands had seized momentum, and Brazil never fully recovered.

Fifteen minutes later, Sneijder headed in a corner kick for a second goal. The game finished 2–1 Netherlands.

The victory sent the Dutch on to a lively semifinal against Uruguay, then the finals against Spain. There they were outclassed and outplayed. Spain lifted the World Cup trophy. It was a deserving win for *La Roja*, the Red, many of them Kaká's teammates from Real Madrid.

But Brazil was heartbroken. Dunga was fired three days after the loss. His experiment with the team was over. It was only the third time in history that Brazil failed to reach the finals in consecutive World Cups.

Kaká felt the loss deeply. This had been his team. He was its leader and superstar. And together the team had not succeeded in reaching its goal.

"It wasn't just me who had expectations but the whole team, and the only way we could fulfill them was by winning the title," a downcast Kaká said after the loss. "No matter when we lose or how, there are always going to be broken dreams. And now that we're not going to win the World Cup, everyone's suffering."

The Seleção would have to wait four more years for another chance. And none of these players would be guaranteed another opportunity, especially with Brazil's always deep pool of rising young players. This had been Kaká's third World Cup—an incredible accomplishment. Would he get another chance to represent his country?

"I don't know what lies ahead. This is a difficult moment in my life and my career," he said. "I have a very strong bond with the national team, and this is the toughest situation I've had to face. I have to sit down and have a think about my life and my career."

## World Cup 2010 Awards

Golden Ball (Most Outstanding Player): Diego Forlan, Uruguay

Golden Boot (Top Scorer): Tomas Mueller, Germany — 5 goals, 3 assists

Golden Glove (Top Goalkeeper): Iker Casillas, Spain

Best Young Player Award: Tomas Mueller, Germany

Fair Play Award: Spain

Final Standings:

- Winner: Spain
- Runner-up: Netherlands
- Third: Germany
- Fourth: Uruguay

# Sidelined by Surgery

Kaká needed surgery. He had played with pain in his left knee during the World Cup, and it worsened when he returned to Real Madrid's training camp shortly afterward. The doctor, Marc Martens, made big news when he said, "It could have finished his career because it's a very serious injury. It could have destroyed him."

Kaká disagreed. "Martens is a great professional, but he raised the alarm," Kaká said. "He exaggerated a lot." Especially about how bad Kaká's pain had been during the World Cup.

What was certain was that the surgery went well—that was good. But it was bad that recovery would take at least three or four months. Kaká was hopeful that repairing his knee would pay off.

"I will be the best in the world again," he said. "Today it's difficult to say this, but I think I'm going to be successful with Real Madrid. I had the operation to be No. 1 again."

But Kaká would miss many games—even more than during last season. It was a blow to the team. Still, expectations in Madrid were higher than ever for the new season. They even had a new coach, José Mourinho.

Mourinho was Real Madrid's eleventh coach in the last seven years. And the club would pay him $12 million a year, the highest salary of any coach in any sport on the planet.

That was huge money, but Mourinho had done what Real wanted to do: win the Champions League. In fact, Mourinho had won Europe's grand prize with two different teams: Portugal's Porto in 2004 and Italy's Inter Milan in 2010. He led England's Chelsea to the semifinals twice in between. Meanwhile, it had been since 2002 that Real Madrid had hoisted that trophy—much too long for their liking. They hadn't even made it to the quarterfinals since 2004.

Mourinho's record earned him respect from many players and coaches. Some called him the best coach in the world. But the Portuguese manager's brash style often earned him critics. He dueled with the press, looked for any psychological edge to motivate his team or disrupt opponents, and taunted other teams in celebrations of goals or victories. His ego seemed to match his paycheck.

Mourinho had been nicknamed "The Special One" after his first press conference as the coach of Chelsea in 2004. Though Mourinho had used the phrase to defend his credentials, the English media seemed to exaggerate his tone. But the nickname stuck. Would the Special One bring a special season to Madrid?

"I have a lot of confidence in myself and my ability as a coach," Mourinho said when he arrived.

Besides the new coach, new players came to Madrid, including big signings Ángel Di María, Ricardo Carvalho, Sami Khedira, and Mesut Özil. Özil had a breakout World Cup, helping lead Germany to the semifinals before losing to Spain. The twenty-two-year-old was an attacking midfielder similar to Kaká. Media speculated that he would replace Madrid's injured Brazilian. But the new coach stuck by Kaká—sort of.

"If we lose him for some time it's no drama," Mourinho said. "We have other players and that's it, but he's one of the best players in the world."

The team looked tough, and overtook first place in La Liga by October. They didn't lose any of the first nineteen games. Then came the first match against archrival Barcelona. The 0–5 loss to Barca was a game Madrid wanted to forget. Lionel Messi, Xavi Hernández, Andrés Iniesta, and the rest of the Blaugrana kept the ball away from Madrid for most of the game. It was Mourinho's worst loss ever as a coach. And Barcelona overtook the lead in La Liga.

Better news came to Madrid a couple weeks later when Kaká returned to training with the team. He would slowly have to build back his fitness and earn his way back into the starting lineup, especially with Özil playing well ahead of him. But it was good to be back.

On January 3, 2011, Kaká returned to competition when he substituted in for the final fifteen minutes against Getafe. A week later he scored his first goal of the season against Villareal. The 4–2 win meant Madrid trailed Barcelona by two points for the La Liga lead. On February 6, Kaká returned to the starting lineup against Real Sociedad.

Then another setback came at the end of February. Kaká reinjured his left knee. Surgery to drain it of fluid meant he would miss another two weeks. The team experienced frustration as well, losing other players such as forward Gonzalo Higuaín and falling to eight points behind Barcelona. Maybe there was still time to turn things around.

Kaká got a big confidence boost in April, when he started and scored twice against Athletic Bilbao.

"I need to work hard to enjoy football again. The only problem was with my knee, which limited me from playing all out," Kaká said after that game. "I have to work hard in this final stretch of the season. I hope to have fun playing football. I feel like I owe it to Real Madrid, and the fact that I haven't fulfilled expectations bothers me."

That didn't keep Kaká from having fun celebrating his two goals on April 23 by putting the ball under his jersey like he was pregnant. Immediately after the game, he flew to São Paulo, Brazil. On the way, he got special permission to call the hospital, and he learned that Caroline had given birth to their daughter, Isabella Celico Leite. Kaká's birthday was the day before, and Easter Sunday was the next day. Caroline posted on her

Kaká and his wife, Carol Celico, pose with their newborn baby
Isabella who was born in Sao Paulo, April 23, 2011.

HO/Marucia Kintschev/Reuters/Landov

social media, "She is a little angel, and I am more in love every minute! I just have to thank God for the privilege of being a mother again!" Soon after, the Brazilian magazine *Istoé Gente* pictured the whole family on its cover, announcing "Kaká's princess."

The new father returned to the field for the critical final six weeks of the season. That stretch featured four critical matches against Barcelona. Once again, all of Madrid's hopes for titles in La Liga, the Copa del Rey, and the Champions League hinged on the Clásicos.

First came the La Liga matchup at home in the Bernabeu. The heated duel shifted early in the second half when Raul Albiol was red-carded in the penalty box. Messi gave Barca the 1–0 lead, and Madrid faced the uphill battle of coming back with only ten men. But the Whites continued to fight and shifted into more of an attacking mode when Özil entered the game. In the eighty-third minute, Barca's Dani Alves fouled Marcelo in the box. Cristiano Ronaldo converted the penalty kick. The game finished in a 1–1 tie. It would be next to impossible for Madrid to overtake Barca now for the La Liga title, but the tie was a great improvement over Madrid's early season 0–5 loss. It felt like a moral victory for Madrid—especially with what was at stake in the next three Clásicos.

Four days later, Madrid and Barcelona squared off in the finals of the Copa del Rey. Madrid sent the speedy Cristiano Ronaldo, Di Maria, and Özil on attack. Madrid came closest to scoring, but the intense battle remained scoreless all the way through. Finally, in overtime

Ronaldo leaped and headed in the goal that proved to be the winner.

It was Madrid's first King's Cup title in seventeen years—and the first trophy for Kaká, Cristiano Ronaldo, Mourinho, and the other new Galacticos at Madrid. Ironically, Sergio Ramos accidentally dropped the large silver cup off of the bus during the team's victory parade. The bus ran over it before it could stop. Police retrieved it and returned the trophy to the driver.

Next up in the Clásico marathon was the two-game Champions League duel. Mourinho had succeeded in guiding Real Madrid to the semifinals, farther than the team had been in years.

One week after the Copa del Rey final, the giants clashed in the Bernabeu. Both teams threatened for goals, but the first half ended scoreless. Tension was high, and players got into a scuffle as they walked to the locker rooms. Madrid had played defensively the first half, but began to attack more after halftime. Los Blancos were building momentum when defender Pepe was ejected with a red card. Mourinho was also ejected for his protests to the referee. Now Barcelona wore down the short-sided Madrid, and Lionel Messi took over. He scored two goals in the final fifteen minutes to give Barcelona a 2–0 victory and lead in the series.

Madrid needed to win the next meeting by more than two goals to advance. Kaká and Higuaín were back in the starting lineup for attacking power. But Barcelona took control early. Madrid's captain and goalkeeper Iker Casillas made save after save. Higuaín put a shot into

Barca's net shortly after halftime, but the referee disallowed it because he had already whistled a foul. A few minutes later, Barca's Pedro Rodriguez scored. Marcelo answered for Madrid ten minutes later. The game ended 1–1, but Barcelona won the Champions League semis by the combined 3–1 score.

Barcelona officially won La Liga several days later. They also went on to win the Champions League over Manchester United. The archrivals were on a roll.

Madrid, on the other hand, had improved its performance over the previous season, but the team's goals were unfulfilled.

A bright spot came for Kaká in the following summer, when Brazil's new coach, Mano Menezes, invited him back to join the Seleção for some international friendlies. Kaká was honored but declined so he could rest his knee and fully recover. He had unfinished business at Madrid and needed to be at full strength once again.

**José Mourinho**

Mourinho worked his way into professional coaching in his homeland, Portugal. He began as an interpreter, then became an assistant at Sporting CP and then FC Porto. He served as an assistant at Barcelona and then was hired as head coach of the Portuguese club Benfica in 2000. Since then he has assembled an impressive record. He has won league titles in Portugal, England, Italy, and Spain. And he has won the UEFA Champions League with two clubs: Portugal's Porto and Italy's

Internazionale, or Inter Milan. In 2010, Mourinho was the first to win the FIFA Ballon d'Or Best Coach Award. Due to his outspoken and proud style, controversy often surrounds "The Special One."

## Lionel Messi

Messi has widely been considered the best player in the world in recent years. Some say he is the greatest ever. In 2013, he became the first player in history to win four Ballon d'Or awards for World Player of the Year.

Messi has played his whole career for Barcelona. He moved from his home country, Argentina, and entered the club's youth academy, La Masia, when he was fourteen. The boy was also small and had a growth hormone deficiency that kept him from growing. Barcelona paid for the medical treatments that helped his body grow normally. Still only five-feet, seven-inches tall, Messi is known as *La Pulga*, the Flea, for his ability to dart around opponents, avoid being knocked over, or bounce back up — all while keeping the ball with amazing dribbling ability.

In 2012-2013, Messi scored 91 goals in all competitions and broke the forty-year-old record held by Germany's Gerd Muller. Messi has won every club trophy possible, including six La Liga and three Champions League titles. The world will be watching in 2014 to see if Messi can bring Argentina a World Cup championship.

# 21

# Ups and Downs – For Kaká and Club

Kaká knew he needed to rest and heal completely. Good health and fitness are absolutely vital to any professional athlete. To be able to push for top performance against the best in the world requires the body to work at peak capacity, game after game, practice after daily practice. Any injury can interrupt the flow, and trying to come back is tricky. Go hard too soon, and risk reinjury that might be even worse. Wait too long, and lose your starting spot to other players.

Kaká had ridden the injury roller coaster during the past two seasons. He was ready to show what he could do consistently at Real Madrid. But would he get the chance? The pattern of the next two seasons would be constant trade rumors, bouncing in and out of the lineup, and growing unrest club wide.

There is always a lot of talk in the media about which

players and teams will go where. It's especially true during the European summer off-season and January transfer window, when clubs are allowed to hire or trade players. Real Madrid's midfield was crowded with talent. José Mourinho seemed to favor other players ahead of Kaká, but other teams were interested in him.

Would Kaká remain at Madrid? Rumors of a transfer flew. Media reports suggested moves to many top European clubs: England's Chelsea, Paris Saint Germaine, Turkey's Galatasaray, England's Tottenham, and always his former club AC Milan. The player always insisted he wanted to stay, and the coach and club president publically said they wanted to keep him.

As the 2011–2012 season got underway, Kaká appeared to be playing at his pre-injury level. At the end of September, he played one of his finest games since coming to Madrid. And it was an important one, a Champions League group game against the Dutch powerhouse Ajax. Kaká started the game, scored one goal, and assisted on another in the 3–0 victory. He was named Man of the Match for his efforts.

"For those of us who have kept faith in him, seeing the look of happiness he has had on his face for a while now is very satisfying," said Madrid's assistant coach Aitor Karanka after the game. "A great player like him, and considering what he has been through, deserves to be happy again."

Team captain Iker Casillas added his support but also gave a reminder of the media's fickleness. "We know what a class player and person he is, and we have faith in him. He is committed to himself, to his teammates, and to the team," Casillas said. "We want him to be what he was before, but we know what the press is like. If he has a less brilliant match, he'll be criticized again."

Kaká remained gracious and repeated his desire to win for Madrid. "I am indebted to Real Madrid and the club," he said. "It would be very easy to have gone, but that is why I raised my game. I have a dream of winning with Madrid which I want to realize."

The dream appeared to be back on track. A month later, Kaká was officially called up to play for Brazil for the first time since the World Cup. "I had always said, and he was aware of it, that if [Kaká] returned to form and he started to play regularly again, he would return to the team," Brazil's coach Mano Menezes said. "This is a good opportunity for that to happen."

"Very happy with the call to return to Brazilian National Team," Kaká shared on Facebook and Twitter. "After a long period away, the thrill of being back is great. Thank you all that as I waited for this moment. #GlorytoGod"

A week later, injury struck again, another leg muscle injury. It meant that he would miss several weeks of playing, including the games for Brazil.

Was this injury the last straw for Mourinho? Media outlets buzzed with rumors that Madrid was now willing to sell its Brazilian star. But no moves were made.

Real Madrid controlled La Liga for most of the 2011–2012 season and claimed the league title, nine points ahead of Barcelona. Madrid's 100 points set a La Liga season record.

But Los Blancos couldn't make it past the semifinals in the Champions League. This time they fell to Bayern Munich of Germany. The loss was a heartbreaker on penalty kicks. Bayern missed two. But Cristiano Ronaldo and Kaká both missed their shots. It was all over when Madrid's Sergio Ramos sent his penalty kick screaming high over the bar.

Madrid met a similar fate in the following year's Champions League—losing to another German club in the semifinals. In 2013, it was Borussia Dortmund who knocked out Los Merengues, though it wasn't as close. Dortmund took a big lead with a 4–1 first-leg victory, and Madrid's 2–0 win in the second match wasn't enough.

The Champions loss was the final frustration in that long and controversial season at Madrid. The La Liga title was long lost, and Madrid finished in second, fifteen points behind champion Barcelona. Even the Copa del Rey was lost in the final to Atlético Madrid.

Unrest had been brewing in and around the Bernabeu all year. Back in the early season, Cristiano Ronaldo told reporters after a victory, "I'm sad because of a professional issue and the club know why. That's why I didn't celebrate the goals, because I'm not happy. The people [at the club] know why."

He didn't give any details.

A rift opened between Mourinho and long-time Madrid players such as Iker Casillas and Sergio Ramos. Some of it was fueled by Mourinho's decision to bench goalkeeper Casillas, the captain and team leader. By

December, it was clear that the relationship between Mourinho and club president Florentino Pérez had broken down. And by May, there was a feud in the press between Mourinho and defender Pepe. Mourinho made many not-so-subtle comments pointing to his exit at the end of the season. He wanted out. The club wanted him out too.

In the meantime, Mourinho decided who played, and Kaká wasn't on his favorites list, even when the Brazilian put in a stellar performance like another against Ajax in Champions League group play in October 2012. "What has made Mourinho so hostile to Kaká's presence at the Bernabeu?" asked Rob Train, a sportswriter who covers Real Madrid for ESPN.

Through it all, Kaká stayed out of the public feuds and refused to criticize his coach. He tried to stay positive and continued to work hard to win back a starting role.

"I am going to keep doing my part of the work," Kaká said early in the season. "My motivation will be to regain confidence, both my own and that of Mourinho. I can only do that, training in the morning and in the afternoon."

He knew it would take perseverance.

"The season is very long, and maybe I will have an opportunity," he added. "I need to have patience."

Throughout the year, Kaká tweeted and posted Bible verses to Facebook, such as Colossians 3:23, "Whatever you do, work at it with all your heart, as working for the Lord, not for human masters"; and Proverbs 3:5–6, "Trust in the Lord with all your heart and lean not on your own understanding." They seemed like reminders to himself as he looked for strength from God as much as encouragement for his VIFs, or Very Important Followers, as he calls them.

Kaká certainly didn't like everything that happened during the difficult 2011–2012 and 2012–2013 seasons, but he knew the challenges would help him grow. "To pass from being a protagonist to being, 'a normal player,' is tough, but it has helped me to mature on a personal and professional level," he said.

He would continue to persevere.

## Mano Menezes

Menezes had a long and successful coaching career in Brazil before taking over as head of the Seleção from 2010 to 2012. He had served as head coach for Grêmio, Corinthians, and several other clubs. In 2013 he was hired to lead Flamengo in Rio de Janeiro, Brazil's most popular professional team.

## World's Most Valuable Soccer Teams

Each year since 2004, *Forbes*, the American business magazine, has tracked and listed the richest and most valuable soccer clubs in the world. Here are the top results and current values from 2013:
1. Real Madrid, $3.3 billion
2. Manchester United, $3.17 billion
3. Barcelona, $2.6 billion
4. Arsenal, $1.3 billion
5. Bayern Munich, $1.3 billion

# Hope

The dream was still alive! Kaká never gave up hope of playing for his country in the World Cup again, no matter how bad the struggles got at Real Madrid. Brazil would host the massive event in 2014. To play in the gold jersey — to hoist the golden trophy — to give glory to God and celebrate with millions of soccer-mad Brazilians would be a dream come true. The goal drove Kaká to continue giving his best day after day.

In September 2012, he got a call from the national team. Brazil wanted him back for a pair of friendlies against Iraq and Japan.

"We need players as experienced as Kaká is with the national team," Coach Mano Menezes said. "We think that he will come here and show that he has improved. We know that this season will be key for him so we can start counting on him as a national team player again in the future."

"What a wonderful day!!! Called up to the Brasilian national team and qualified for the quarter finals of the Champions!" Kaká tweeted. "What a joy! I want to thank all those who cheer for these achievements. #tksvifs"

And he gave Brazilians plenty to cheer about in a triumphant return against Iraq. The Seleção dominated in a 6–0 victory. Kaká scored one solo goal on a break-away, and he created a beautiful assist to set up another goal for Oscar. Iraq was a heavy underdog, but Japan should prove to be a tougher test, especially after coming off a surprise victory over powerful France.

Brazil didn't let that bother them. They rolled past the Blue Samurai 4–0. Again Kaká scored and created opportunities. His goal came in the 76th minute when he broke free of a defender and slotted a low shot past the goalkeeper. Perhaps more importantly, Kaká provided a solid link between fellow midfielder Oscar and attackers Neymar and Hulk.

Kaká featured in the next game against Colombia, but Brazil could only muster a 1–1 tie. The team had struggled earlier in the year against traditional top teams such as Argentina, and losing the 2012 Olympics to Mexico in the finals the previous summer had been considered a failure. The nation's expectations were as high as ever. So when Luiz Felipe Scolari became available, Brazil fired Menezes and hired Scolari in November 2012. Felipão, or Big Phil, was the last coach to lead the

Seleção to a World Cup championship in 2002. He was hired to do it again.

But what changes would he make?

He left Kaká off his twenty-man roster in his first match, a friendly against England that the team lost 1–2. Brazil's soccer experts were puzzled. "It is incomprehensible to me that Scolari left Kaká out," said Juca Kfouri, one of Brazil's leading sports commentators. "As much as he hasn't played regularly for Real Madrid he is the kind of player who works his socks off for the national team."

It seemed that Kaká's national team quest would be similar to his efforts at Real Madrid. There too, even though he wasn't getting much playing time from Mourinho, he was putting in high caliber performances when he got the chance. Still, he pressed on. "Stay positive. Stay fighting. Stay brave. Stay ambitious. Stay focused. Stay strong... Mentality is everything," read a photo he posted on Instagram with the text, "Confidence in what we hope for and assurance about what we do not see. #faith #JC #nevergiveup"

In March, Felipão brought Kaká back for games against Russia and Italy. With 83 caps, Kaká was the most experienced member of the young squad. Both results were ties.

The big news was the roster for the Confederations Cup, the World Cup warm-up tournament held in Brazil in June 2013. When the list of twenty-three players was announced in May, Scolari's intention was clear: He was putting all the nation's hopes on a young team. Veterans who he had been looking at in the squad, including Kaká and Ronaldinho, were left out.

Many Brazilians, fans and media, were concerned. No one doubted the extraordinary skills of the likes of Neymar and Oscar, but were they ready to carry the team on their own? Felipão was going to find out.

Brazil had to be considered a favorite at home, but all the pundits had reservations about the squad's lack of experience. After all, the competition consisted of the champion from each continent, including current world ruler and reigning World Cup champion, Spain.

The Canarinho began putting any fears to rest right away. They collected all nine possible points with three wins during the opening group round. Brazil out-performed each progressive opponent, beating Japan, Mexico, and Italy solidly—and excitingly.

Off the field, millions of Brazilians took to the streets to protest unfair practices by their government, such as raising the fees of public transportation and spending millions on new stadiums instead of helping the nation's lower class. Many players supported their countrymen's exercise of democratic freedom and called for the people and the police to stay peaceful.

On the field, the semifinals brought a matchup of South American rivals: Brazil versus Uruguay. Again Brazil came out on top. Elsewhere European powers squared off, and Spain bested Italy in a penalty kick shootout. The world would be getting a dream final: Brazil versus Spain.

The thrilling game did not disappoint. It was no surprise that Spain edged Brazil in total possession of the ball. The Spaniards' ability to endlessly connect short passes and wear down opponents is unmatched by any team in the world. And it wasn't a total surprise that Brazil could come out victorious. What was surprising was that Brazil won so handily: 3–0.

Brazil celebrated. The young team had delivered, and it had set the stage for the coming World Cup. It was a triumphant moment for Brazil. But did it mean the end of the dream for Kaká?

## Neymar

Neymar da Silva Santos Junior is one of the world's best young rising stars. Already he is compared to Pelé and Lionel Messi. In 2011, the then-nineteen-year-old won the South American Footballer of the Year Award. That same year he won the FIFA Puskás Award for the most beautiful goal. Neymar began his professional career in Brazil, playing for Santos. In 2013 he signed a contract with Barcelona. Known for his speed, creative dribbling, and electric scoring, Neymar will carry the expectations to lead Brazil in the 2014 World Cup.

## Brazil 2014

Dates: June 12 – July 13, 2014
Official slogan: All in one rhythm. *Juntos num só ritmo* in Portuguese.
Mascot: Fuleco, a Brazilian three-banded armadillo
Host cities: twelve, including São Paulo, which will host the opening match, and Rio de Janeiro, which will host the final

# Toward the Goal

New hope rose on the horizon. José Mourinho was leaving Real Madrid to return to Chelsea in England's Premiere League. The move was no surprise, and it became official as La Liga wrapped up in May 2013. His replacement would be Carlo Ancelotti—the coach who had led Kaká and AC Milan to the top of Italy and of the Champions League several years earlier.

Ancelotti was heralded as a peacemaker by the press. Like Mourinho, Ancelotti brought an impressive list of coaching accomplishments. The Italian had won two Champions League titles, two European Super Cups, a Club World Cup, and league championships in Italy, England, and France. But his calm style was very different from Mourinho's brash ways. Madridistas hoped that Ancelotti would bring positive changes after Real Madrid's tumultuous several previous years.

His arrival also meant that Kaká might get a more fair chance in Madrid, even with its always crowded midfield. As the usual summer transfer rumors swirled, Kaká told reporters, "I have a contract with Real Madrid, and we have got a new coach. I have had positive communication with Carlo Ancelotti, and I will stay."

Ancelotti indicated the same. As he met with Madrid's executive leadership, he asked about Kaká. "The Italian knitted his brows in puzzlement, asking whether Kaká had caused any trouble," Spain's largest sports newspaper, *Marca*, reported. "As he expected, the reply was in the negative. He was told that the Brazilian has been a model professional, never uttering a word out of turn or putting a foot out of line, breaking his neck to try to recover his form and showing all the enthusiasm of a fresh-faced youngster when given a rare first-team run-out."

Ancelotti made it clear that he wanted Kaká to stay and that he would give the Brazilian a clean slate. Real Madrid's president Pérez also gave clear support to Kaká when he told reporters, "Kaká is a phenomenon, but he got injured in the last World Cup and had to have an operation on his knee. Then [Mesut] Özil arrived and took his place in the team from him, but he is still one of the greats of the game. He is the second most followed footballer on Twitter, after Cristiano Ronaldo. He is charming and excites the fans. I'm optimistic that, under Ancelotti, who knows him very well, he can be the same magical Kaká again that we signed."

But the world of professional sports changes fast. Just as the new season was getting underway, news broke

Kaká hold up his Milan jersey, joining the team again in September 2013.

that Kaká was heading back to AC Milan in Italy. This time it was for real.

"I really want to play," Kaká told Milan Channel. "This is a special year for me because the World Cup is coming up, but now I've got to do well with Milan. I was very sorry to leave, but now it's even more special to come back."

Milan fans cheered the homecoming of their former star. After all, Kaká enjoyed his most successful years with the club. The players and club leaders welcomed him back with open arms too, even making Kaká vice-captain of the team as soon as he returned. They knew that Kaká would be a valuable veteran who could help lead and create plays for the young Rossoneri. "It is a new situation for me though," Kaká said. "I now have a different role here, to help the youngsters here as I was helped by great champions in the past."

And Kaká knows that much of his hope for reaching the World Cup depends on getting valuable playing time with his club. Around the same time, he found another ray of hope when Felipe Scolari told the press he wasn't ruling anyone out of the Brazilian team yet for the World Cup.

"We will keep an eye on every Brazilian player, in Europe and in Brazil, to ensure the best players will be included in the national team in 2014," Felipão said.

Kaká knows reaching the field at the Maracanã takes a great deal of hard work, determination, perseverance, patience, and faith. But he has never been afraid of any of those traits.

"Scolari said the door of the national team is still open," he said. "There is more than a year to go before the World Cup, and the season is just starting. From my heart, I hope I can be playing in the World Cup next year."

Whether he returns to the World Cup or not, Kaká continues to influence millions of fans around the world. In April 2012 he became the first athlete on the planet to pass 10 million followers on Twitter. He describes himself in his profile there as a "Christian, husband, and father who loves football." And he frequently sends messages in English, Portuguese, Spanish, and Italian. Kaká's Facebook friends number near 25 million.

Kaká wearing ancient Chinese clothing plays Cuju, an ancient Chinese football, in front of the National Stadium on July 2, 2013 in Beijing, China.

ChinaFotoPress via Getty Images

Beyond the millions of social media VIFs, he encourages people around the world through media interviews and international visits. He takes every opportunity to speak about his love for Jesus everywhere, from his own video, *The Rhythm of My Game*, to China and beyond.

"I bring the Bible with me at all times, which is my belief," he said. "No matter in my soccer career or other aspects of my life, no matter during hard time or good situations, it is a spiritual support for me, an essential support."

He delivered a similar message in his homeland, during My Hope Brazil, a 2008 Billy Graham Evangelistic Association event. "I have been named the best soccer player in the world," he said. "This for me was a great honor. But the greatest honor is serving Jesus Christ, because he gives me hope."

It's not surprising that Kaká has expressed the desire to study theology when he eventually retires from professional soccer. "I want to be an evangelical pastor," he told *GQ Italy*. "It is not easy to apply things written thousands of years ago. But that is the job of a good shepherd."

Most important, Kaká continues to back up his words. He still works with the United Nations World Food Program to bring nourishment and opportunity to children in the world's poorest areas. He serves as a spokesperson for the Special Olympics. And he works with several Brazilian charities and ministries, including GRAACC, which translates to Support Group for Children and Adolescents with Cancer.

Kaká is deeply devoted to his family. You can see him on the field making an L and I with his hands—for Luca and Isabella. You can hear him singing with Caroline on the self-titled Christian pop album she recorded in 2010. Together they sing "*Presente de Deus,*" or "Gift of God," the song Kaká wrote Caroline for their wedding.

Kaká's schedule is demanding between games, practices, and appearances for his club and sponsors. Those commitments—especially games on the road—can keep him away from home, but the family loves to travel together too. And Kaká loves to play with Luca and Isabella.

"When he's at home, he's always with them," Caroline said. "He likes to play, jump on the bed and make a tent with the sheets and pillows for Luca. He's a great dad."

"As a parent I want to pass on to my children the values that I believe are correct, that they have a great love for God and for all people," Kaká said on his website.

Blending his faith and sport has always been natural for Kaká, in good times and bad. Either way, Kaká points attention to God. And either way, he looks to God for strength, especially when times are challenging.

"I'm learning from God every day," he said in China. "In fact, God has taught me a lot. For example, I learned that life does not always go well. There is the time of joyful. There is the time of facing difficulties. No matter how, we need try to overcome them."

As an athlete, he understands that defeat comes with victory — and that there is more to both than a simple score in a game and in life. "God really has a way, He has a purpose. The Bible says that all things work together for the good of those who love the Lord. So at the end of the day, this is a great truth," Kaká said. "I may go through moments of defeats, moments that may cause me to think, to have the feeling of failure, but which have really contributed for the will of God to be done in my life and for that will to be good, perfect, and pleasant."

Whether he is accepting awards or fighting to regain his starting position, Kaká remains committed to seeking God's purpose and to working hard and improving. His sharp competitive drive has never faded even though he has accomplished so much. After his Italian Scudetto and World Player of the Year awards in 2007, he said, "My goal now is to win everything twice."

The road has been hard and filled with obstacles, but more prizes are still possible. Another World Cup title with the Brazilians at home during summer 2014 is still possible. And the star-studded group at AC Milan remains within striking range of Serie A and Champions League titles.

Goals on the field have helped to secure Kaká's legacy. But setting goals off the field have always been a motivating force. He quickly achieved the original ten goals he made while healing from his life-threatening neck injury. Then he continued to set—and accomplish—new goals, laying out clear plans of where he wanted to go and working daily to get there.

"I started kicking the ball just for fun," Kaká told *The Telegraph*. "But little by little I fell in love with the game and thought about the possibility of becoming a professional player. In the end I have reached places I had never dreamed of getting to."

One could say Kaká's goals have paved the successful road he has traveled. And the road continues. What additional soccer feats will it lead Kaká to? Only time will tell. But along the way, the watching world will continue to gain motivation and inspiration from the beaming Brazilian always pressing forward, elegantly executing the dance between man and ball, embracing gracefully his role as a world ambassador of the beautiful game, and giving credit where it is ultimately due.

"More than anything else, I need Jesus in my life,"

Kaká said. "I am successful in my financial life and in my professional life, but all this has come from God and is a gift of grace from him for my life. I will never stop following him."

And with that, he presses on—always toward the goal.

# Acknowledgments

Special thanks to the following people who helped to make this book possible. Your insights, perspectives, assistance, and contributions are deeply appreciated:

Marcelo Saragosa, Eduard Cauich, Amy Hanson, Brett Honeycutt, Alex Marestaing, LaSal Miller, Lou Smith, Gary Booker, David McCasland, David Shrift, Rebecca Levine, Annette Bourland, Kim Childress, Kathleen Kerr, Kris Nelson, and Kim Tanner.

# Sources

## Bibliography

de Pauli, Andrea, "'We Have Neared Perfection' Kaká Reflects on Milan's Champions League of Triumph," *Sports Illustrated*, 30 July 2007.

Faillaci, Sara, "Kaká and the Sex of Angels," *Vanity Fair*, 14 June 2007.

*The Prize: Quest for the Ultimate Goal*, Athletes in Action and The Film Foundry, 2006.

## Websites

"Alves Hails Brazilian Flair," *FIFA*, 11 June 2010. *http://www.fifa.com* (accessed September 10, 2013).

"Ancelotti Shattered After Defeat," *BBC Sport*, 25 May 2005. *http://news.bbc.co.uk* (accessed September 10, 2013).

"A Princesa de Kaká," *Istoé Gente*, 2 May 2011. *http://issuu.com/editora3/docs/istoegente_607* (accessed September 10, 2013).

Associated Press, "Brazil Recalls Kaká to Face Iraq, Japan," *ESPN FC*, 27 September 2012. *http://espnfc.com* (accessed September 10, 2013).

Associated Press, "Kaká Says Doctor 'Exaggerated'," *ESPN*, 13 August 2010. *http://espn.go.com* (accessed September 10, 2013).

Associated Press, "Kaká Takes Significant Pay Cut to Return to AC Milan," *Sports Illustrated*, 2 September, 2013. *http://sportsillustrated.cnn.com* (accessed October 18, 2013).

Bellos, Alex, "How Privileged Kaká Made Most of Luck to Become Brazil's Master of Magic: Middle-class Midfielder is Tipped to Be Champions' Best Performer On and Off Pitch," *Guardian* (England), 17 June 2006. *http://www.guardian.co.uk* (accessed September 10, 2013).

"Brazil Crowned World Champions," *BBC Sport*, 30 June 2002. *http://news.bbc.co.uk* (accessed September 10, 2013).

"Brazil Lick Their Wounds," *FIFA*, 3 July 2010. *www.fifa.com* (accessed September 10, 2013).

"Can Brazil Provide Six Appeal?" *FIFA*, 23 May 2010. *www.fifa.com* (accessed September 10, 2013).

"Carol Celico's Interview," *Kakafans.net*, 25 August 2011. *http://www.kakafans.net/?p=5583*Kaká (accessed September 10, 2013).

Castles, Duncan, "Meet Brazil's Rooney... Without the Swearing and the Sex Scandals," *Daily Mail* (London), 21 February 2005. *http://www.dailymail.co.uk* (accessed September 10, 2013).

Corrigan, Dermot, "Kaká: We'll support Ronaldo," *ESPN FC*, 3 September 2012. *http://espnfc.com* (accessed September 10, 2013).

"Dunga Out to Fill Kaká Void," *FIFA*, 24 June 2010. *www.fifa.com* (accessed September 10, 2013).

"Dunga Reveals Unwavering Belief," *FIFA*, 29 June 2009. *http://www.fifa.com* (accessed September 10, 2013).

"Dunga: We're Getting Better," *FIFA*, 28 June 2010. *www.fifa.com* (accessed September 10, 2013).

Duarte, Fernando, "Kaká: Real Outcast, Selecao Savior?" *ESPN FC*, 23 January 2013. *http://espnfc.com* (accessed September 10, 2013).

Elkington, Mark and Justin Palmer, "Soccer-Kaká Sees 'Clasico' as Chance to Revive his Real Career," *Reuters*, 1 March 2013. *http://uk.reuters.com* (accessed September 10, 2013).

ESPN Soccernet Staff, "Kaká earns Brazil call-up," *ESPN FC*, 28 October 2011. *http://espnfc.com* (accessed September 10, 2013).

ESPN Staff, "Kaká Hoping to Stay On at Madrid," *ESPN FC*, 2 July 2013. *http://espnfc.com* (accessed September 10, 2013).

ESPN Soccernet Staff, "Kaká takes the plaudits," *ESPN FC*, 28 September 2011. *http://espnfc. com* (accessed September 10, 2013).

ESPN Staff, "Ronaldo 'not happy' with Madrid," *ESPN FC*, 3 September 2012. *http://espnfc. com* (accessed September 10, 2013).

Fenn, Alec, "Kaká: I Will Stay at Real Madrid," *Yahoo Sports*, 2 July 2013. *http://sports.yahoo. com* (accessed September 10, 2013).

Football Espana Staff, "Kaká: I'd Lost My Desire in Madrid," Football Espana, 5 September 2013. *http:// www.football-espana.net* (accessed October 18, 2013).

Geromel, Ricardo, "All You Need to Know About Sao Paulo, Brazil's Largest City," *Forbes*, 12 July 2013. *http://www.forbes.com* (accessed September 10, 2013).

Hanson, Amy (translator),"Quero ganhar tudo duas vezes," *Veja*, 19 December 2007. *http:// veja.abril.com.br/191207/p_128.shtml* (accessed September 10, 2013).

Hunter, Graham, "It's Now or Never For Real Madrid," *ESPN*, 16 March 2011. *http://espn. go.com* (accessed September 10, 2013).

John, Paula, "Kaká Tells Fans in China: God Has Taught Me A Lot," *Christian Post*, 5 July 2013. *http://ipost.christianpost.com* (accessed September 10, 2013).

Kaká, 23 February 2013. *http://instagram.com/Kaka* (accessed September 10, 2013).

Kaká, *Twitter*, *https://twitter.com/kaka* (accessed September 10, 2013).

"Kaká Completes Real Madrid Switch," *BBC Sport*, 9 June 2009. *http://news.bbc.co.uk* (accessed September 10, 2013).

"Kaká–Este é o ritmo do meu jogo, Parte 01," *YouTube*, 14 January 2011. *http://www.youtube. com* (accessed September 10, 2013).

"Kaká–Este é o ritmo do meu jogo, Parte 03," *YouTube*, 14 January 2011. *http://www.youtube. com* (accessed September 10, 2013).

"Kaká: I'd Lost My Desire in Madrid," *Football Espana*, 5 September 2013. *http://www.football -espana.net* (accessed October 7, 2013).

"Kaká: Real Madrid Players Must Work Hard," *Independent* (London), 14 July 2009. *http:// www.independent.co.uk* (accessed September 10, 2013).

"Kaká Takes Significant Pay Cut to Return to AC Milan," *Sports Illustrated*, 2 September 2013. *http://sportsillustrated.cnn.com* (accessed October 7, 2013).

"Kaká," Veja Cronologia, http://veja.abril.com.br/cronologia/kaka/index.html (accessed September 10, 2013).

"Kaká Voted FIFPro World Player of the Year," FIFPro Official Award Website, 10 May 2007. *http://worldsl.fifpro.org* (accessed September 10, 2013).

Kvesa, Chris, "Scolari Hints at Possible Ronaldinho and Kaká Recalls," *Goal*, 1 July 2013. *http://www.goal.com* (accessed September 10, 2013).

"La Liga: Real Madrid Sweat on Kaká Fitness," *ESPN FC*, 3 December 2009. www.espnfc.com (accessed September 10, 2013).

Lyttleton, Ben, "Kaká beats Cristiano Ronaldo to Ballon d'Or," *The Telegraph*, 25 November 2007. *http://www.telegraph.co.uk* (accessed September 10, 2013).

"Man City Move for Kaká Collapses," *BBC Sport*, 20 January 2009. *http://news.bbc.co.uk* (accessed September 10, 2013).

Marcotti, Gabriele, "Milan's Kaká is a Brazilian Superstar with Vision But No Vices," *Times Online*, 15 January 2009. *http://www.timesonline.co.uk* (accessed September 10, 2013).

"Minnows Knock Madrid Out of a Cup," *BBC Sport*, 11 November 2009. www.news.bbc.co.uk (accessed September 10, 2013).

Mitten, Andy, "The Golden Boy of a Golden Team," *Independent* (London), 4 June 2006. *http://www.independent.co.uk* (accessed September 10, 2013).

"My Life: Husband and Father," *Kaká*, *http://www.Kakáww.com* (accessed September 10, 2013).

"Nasce a filha de Kaká," Istoé Gente, 23 April 2011. http://www.istoegente.com.br/noticias/gente/nasce-a-filha-de-kaka/ (accessed September 10, 2013).

Ozanian, Mike, "Soccer's Most Valuable Teams: At $3.3 Billion, Real Madrid Knocks Manchester United From Top Spot," *Forbes*, 17 April 2013. *http://www.forbes.com* (accessed September 10, 2013).

"Player to Watch: Kaká is the new 'White Pele,'" *FIFA.com*, 26 May 2004. *http://www.fifa.com* (accessed September 10, 2013).

"Primera Division: Kaká Staying at Spanish Giants Real Madrid," *Sky Sports*, 12 July 2013. *http://www1.skysports.com* (accessed September 10, 2013).

"Q&A: Kaká," *FourFourTwo.com* interview, 15 January 2008. *http://www.fourfourtwo.com/features/kaka* (accessed September 10, 2013).

"Real Madrid Unveil Jose Mourinho as Their New Coach," *BBC Sport*, 31 May 2010, *http://news.bbc.co.uk* (accessed September 10, 2013).

Ricardo Kaká, 5 March 2013. *https://www.facebook.com/Kaká* (accessed September 10, 2013).

Ricardo Kaká, 18 March 2013. *https://www.facebook.com/Kaká* (accessed September 10, 2013).

Ricardo Kaká, 6 May 2013. *https://www.facebook.com/Kaká* (accessed September 10, 2013).

Ricardo Kaká, 27 October 2011. *https://www.facebook.com/Kaká* (accessed September 10, 2013).

Ryan, Mark, "Sunday History Beckons for the World's Greatest Footballer," *Mail Online* (London), 20 May 2007. *http://www.dailymail.co.uk* (accessed September 10, 2013).

Sánchez-Flor, Ulises, "Italian Believes He Can Contribute: Ancelotti Set to Hand Kaká A Lifeline," *Marca*, 7 July 2013. *http://www.marca.com* (accessed September 10, 2013).

"Sao Paulo 2x1 Botafogo–Final do Rio-SP 2001," *YouTube*, 23 September 2011. *www.youtube.com* (accessed September 10, 2013).

Soccernet Staff, "Kaká Injury Could Have Ended His Career–Doctor," *ESPN FC*, 6 August 2010. *http://espnfc.com* (accessed September 10, 2013).

Soccernet Staff, "Kaká Out For Up to Four Months After Knee Surgery," *ESPN FC*, 5 August 2010, *http://espnfc.com* (accessed September 10, 2013).

Soccernet Staff, "Kaká Reflects on Difficult First Season," *ESPN FC*, 27 April 2010. *www.espnfc.com* (accessed September 10, 2013).

*Telegraph* Staff, "Brazil v Ivory Coast: Dunga and Sven-Goran Eriksson Disagree Over Kaká's Red Card," *The Telegraph*, 20 June 2010. *www.telegraph.co.uk* (accessed September 10, 2013).

Temko, Ned, "Kaká: A Footballer of Faith and Fable," *Observer* (England), 18 January 2009. *http://www.guardian.co.uk* (accessed September 10, 2013).

"The Red Diff Interview," *http://www.ricardo-kaka.com/interview_02.php* (accessed September 10, 2013).

Train, Rob, "Kaká still searching for a lifeline," *ESPN FC*, 29 August 2012. *http://espnfc.com* (accessed September 10, 2013).

Wallace, Sam, "How Milan's Prized Asset Became a Class Apart; Kaká's Story Is Not the Usual Brazilian Tale of Rags to Riches," *Independent* (London), 15 January 2009. *http://www.independent.co.uk* (accessed September 10, 2013).

World Bank, "World Development Indicators," Updated July 12, 2013. Google Public Data. http://www.google.com/publicdata/explore?ds=d5bncppjof8f9_&met_y=sp_pop_totl&hl=en&dl=en&idim=country:BRA.